Passage Through India

Other Books by Gary Snyder

PASSAGE THROUGH INDIA

AN EXPANDED AND ILLUSTRATED EDITION

GARY SNYDER

COUNTERPOINT

BERKELEY

Passage through India
Copyright © 1972, 1983, 2014 by Gary Snyder

New preface © 2007 by Gary Snyder

Library of Congress Cataloging-in-Publication Data is available

ISBN-13: 978-1-59376-178-3

All photos taken by Joanne Kyger and Gary Snyder

Originally titled "Now India," this text was first published in somewhat different form in *Caterpillar* No. 19(V:3), Spring 1972.

Book and cover design by Gopa & Ted2, Inc.

COUNTERPOINT
2560 Ninth Street, Suite 318
Berkeley, CA 94710
www.counterpointpress.com

Printed in the United States of America

For Thea Snyder Lowry

This account started as a letter to her.

Contents

Preface to the New Edition (2007)

THIS ACCOUNT comes round again. More photographs now, unpacked from back boxes in the barn and former chickencoop, pretty much still good. Forty-some years later. But I've been back to India since, spending days in Delhi and weeks in Ladakh, Nepal, and up to the Sherpa home country and the trekking route to the foot of Mount Sagarmatha in the land known as the Khumbu.

I've been back a few times to Japan as well. I think a lot about both India and Japan. India anciently belongs with the Occident and the Middle East far more than East Asia. Main population Caucasoid, and at least half of the languages belonging to the same family as Gaelic: Indo-European. "Iran" a version of the word Aryan. Such intelligence, pride, and poverty—India is a developed world, but anciently developed in a different way. Today, its joining the new "developed world" is in some ways a decline.

From those travels in India we returned to Japan. Then as now it was almost a model of what the developed world might be. Though heavy-handed, it sports a capitalism with some remnant regard for family and society, and a strong old morality of social harmony. Japan has great regard for itself, and unfortunately less for the rest of the earth. It is one of the several expressions of the core East Asian powerhouse culture which combines Confucian, Taoist, Buddhist, and Western progress-minded scientistic teachings to come up with a fairly successful somewhat restrained materialism. The U.S.A., from which I now look at both India (*Bharat*) and East Asia, though more powerful and more global, seems less at home in the world.

But this is about India. East of the Indus river, the land that gave us Beginning Linguistics (Pāṇini's grammar) and Beginner's and Ender's mind: the teachings of Shakyamuni the Awakened One. Plus all that yoga practice and devotion to a host of Gods and Goddesses that will cleanse the whole universe of pollution (but it's not time yet). That's the high culture. (Whenever I want to get some help with my software I call up somebody who just happens to live in a place like Bangalore. We talk. I take this to be an after-effect of Pāṇini's great work.)

India has always been a land of spread-out countryside societies and tribal complexities. That still underlies the daily public culture, which has a sanity of its own. We learned to love the street life of India, maddening and illuminating, as we paced along the lanes with our backpacks and tattered maps back then, and it's still done now.

Gary Snyder
January 24, 2007

Preface (1983)

TWENTY YEARS AGO I traveled a half-year in India. I had been living in Japan, studying Buddhism, and felt it was time to see the hearth-land of the Buddha's teachings.
Hinduism and its temple architecture and sculpture also fascinated me. Joanne Kyger
and I set forth in the winter of 1962 with our backpacks and stout shoes, from Mura-
sakino in Kyoto, to travel by French ship, bottom third class to Ceylon. We returned
to Japan in good health; and minds deepened, widened, and saddened by the lessons
of India. I wrote this account out of journals and notes, and sent it to my sister.

We were in advance of the counterculture invasion (which came more from Europe
than the U.S.) and weren't burdened with too many visionary expectations. The
account was published low-key in an issue of *Caterpillar* in the early seventies and
then let be, partly because it seemed the topic of India should be allowed to cool. Now
that most of the pilgrims have returned home (Sweden, Germany, Massachusetts)
we might ask ourselves, what was it about. Whatever answers there might be are all
within paradox-paradigm.

Gandhi stands forth as a twentieth-century Bodhisattva, whose impulses and
actions were only marginally inspired by Hindu India.

The culture that articulated (especially in Jain and Buddhist religions) the most
thoroughgoing philosophy of carefulness with life (Ahiṃsā, non-injury) is a land of
ecological degradation and human difficulty.

Pāṇini's elegant analysis of language (5th century B.C.) lives on in the extraordinary logical and verbal fluency of the Indian intelligentsia—now prepared more thoroughly than anyone else on earth to employ the analytical methods of "deconstruction."

Krishna, whose "real face" appeared to J. Robert Oppenheimer as "brighter than a thousand suns" on the occasion of testing the first atom bomb (as it did to Arjuna on the eve of another military exercise), is now celebrated in U.S. airports; and "thunderclouds the dark blue of Krishna" mount perilously over all human affairs.

I honor India for many things: those neolithic cattle breeders who sang daily songs of love to God and Cow, as a family, and whose singing is echoed even today in the recitation of the Vedas and the sutra-chanting of Los Angeles and Japan. The finest love poetry and love sculpture on earth. Exhaustive meditations on mind and evocation of all the archetypes and images. Peerless music and dance. But most, the spectacle of a high civilization that accomplished art, literature, and ceremony without imposing a narrow version of itself on every tribe and village. Civilization without centralization or monoculture. The caste system as a mode of social organization probably made this possible—with some very unattractive side effects. But those who study the nature of the rise of the centralized state will find India full of surprises. And lastly, no culture but India prior to modern times imagined such a scale of being—light years vast universes, light-year size leaps of time. Dramas of millions of lifetimes reborn. How did they do it? Soma? Visitors from Outer Space? Nah. I think just Big Mind drank in with Himalayan snow-melt rivers and seeing Elephant's ponderous daintiness, and keeping ancient shamanistic sages and forest hermits fed on scraps of food, to hear and respect their solid yoga studies. The Buddha Shakyamuni, one of those, was loved and listened to by cowgirls, traders, and courtesans.

India has had superb times—now fallen a while on hard times. And, beginning to end, irreducible pride. The sharp-tongued, sharp-eyed village men and women, skinny with hard work and never a big fat meal to eat a whole lifetime, live under an eternal sky of stars, and on a beginningless earth. They might need aid-dollars or aid-food, but they don't need or want pity or disgust. An anvil the spirit is pounded finer on, India. Skinny, and flashing eyes.

Gary Snyder
August 16, 40083

Passage Through India

Ghanara Fair, good perch.

I. *The* Cambodge

WE LEFT KYOTO on a cold frosty morning—tenth of December 1961, I think it was—just two days after the end of the big Rohatsu Osesshin at the Daitoku-ji monastery, clear and blue sky—with our rucksacks, but Joanne in high heels because we were going on one of the classier express trains, and she still didn't believe me when I said travel in India would be like camping out. In Tokyo we stayed two days with a young couple I'd known only by correspondence—Clayton Eshleman, a new poet, and his new wife. On the twelfth we took the interurban electric from Tokyo down to Yokohama, cleared through immigration and customs, and walked down this long dock to the *Cambodge* where it was moored alongside—a pretty big ship, all painted white. Up the gangplank, and immediately were transported into a new non-Japanese world. Here was a sudden warm perfumy smell, and perfumy stewards, all talking French, and women stewards with sharp permanent hairdos and thin eyebrow lines like older French women seem to go for. I recollect Joanne getting kind of tangled up with her rucksack and the narrow doors and passageways and becoming sort of rattled—I was immediately uncomfortable because of the warmth of the heated ship when we had just come from unheated Japan, and were wearing heavy winter underwear, and sweaters. A steward led us to our cabins, way forward into cabin class. The change is abrupt, because in tourist class they have wooden doors and trim, and a few carpets, but in cabin class it's all steel doors and steel lockers and steel bunks and rubbertile flooring. But nice and clean. Showed us the dining room, which is all bright yellow and red, recently redone, with bright red plastic-covered chairs and couches along the wall, very cheery and

Opposite: Jack Craig, Ginko, and Neale Hunter on the Cambodge.

happy, with portholes to look out and a music system playing popular music constantly. We unpacked and put our stuff in our lockers—at the last minute in Kyoto I decided to buy a camera and be sure of getting good photos in India, so I bought an Asahi Pentax single-lens reflex 35 mm with f2 lens, and was paranoid about it, hiding it in the back of the locker and putting padlocks where I could and locking the cabin. We were given the freedom of the forward deck so there we stood in the late afternoon as the ship pulled away from the dock and we saw the last of the low glare of Yokohama neon (it's a real port town) turning on as it got dark and we sailed away—not really knowing if we'd ever get back to Japan again, India seeming so remote and scary still.

The first few days on the ship were chilly and rough, lots of people stayed in their cabins. A young couple from Kyoto whom we knew was also on board, Jack Craig (who had come originally from Cupertino, California to study Zen, then through a friend of Al Klyce (who is probably back in San Francisco now with his Japanese wife) met a girl working in a bar, whom he fell for, and after several months of tedious hassling they got married and six months later or so left Japan bound for Hong Kong, and thence India by plane, Europe, and New York, where they are now. Jack's lovely wife Ginko was so miserably seasick she thought she'd perish.

Just before Hong Kong the weather cleared and the water smoothed, and we got a chance to talk to some of our fellow cabin-class tween-deck passengers. One was

Helmut Kugl, a German who had gone off to Australia and worked as a carpenter, then went to Japan for four months, and was now off to India to "find Krishnamurti" because he had picked up a book by Krishnamurti and decided this was what he wanted. Anti-German, and totally against any kind of discipline or authority, but he was only about 24, red-haired and freckly—a perpetual frown of doubt on his brow and constant deep and contradictory philosophical questions—he claimed not to have even finished high school. Hilda Hunt was about 60, divorcée, dressed up in lavender, always having her drink before dinner and always talking about her days on the *New Orleans Times-Picayune* (she "knew Hemingway" when he was living in New Orleans)—wrote verse—and had numerous fantastic stories to tell, but was withal quite sweet—had been visiting some younger relatives who were with the armed services in Japan, and was now on the long trip round to Europe, to visit some more young relatives stationed in Germany.

An Australian named Neale Hunter had done French, Chinese, and Japanese literature at the University of Melbourne, then went to work in the bush for a year or so, took the money and went to Japan, Tokyo—lived for about four months in Shinjuku, Tokyo (a kind of bar and underworld hangout zone of enormous dimensions) then took off for India—fellow who knows about literature, wild life, and for some reason became a converted Catholic and is now trying to reconcile Catholicism and Buddhism to suit himself. Among others were a French couple, early-middle-aged

Hong Kong harbor.

anarchists who live in New Caledonia; a pair of nineteen-year-old American boys from Los Angeles off on a world tour, and a couple of gentle Ceylonese school teachers who played chess all the time and argued their respective religions, Catholic and Buddhist.

Hong Kong: we first off headed for the Japanese Consul and presented our papers, applying for a new visa to Japan. Then walked around on the hillside back of town—Joanne went shopping for a raincoat, and Neale and I went into an old style wineshop and talked to the old men in broken Chinese, sampling from various crocks and getting a little drunk—wandered up and down through the crowded alleys, people hanging all their laundry out the apartment balcony windows, old stained concrete and plaster. New buildings don't seem to last long. Hong Kong so crowded—and barbed wire machine-gun emplacements set up all around. Lively, shopping is a major activity, stores are filled with every conceivable thing, especially luxury. Joanne got a French raincoat—we met back at the ship. The next day Joanne, Neale and I took a bus out to the border—about a 30-mile ride. This is on the mainland side. We got up on a hill and gazed out through pine trees at the Chinese Peoples' Republic—spread out before us, a watery plain with houses here and there—a barbed wire fence along a river at the foot of the hill showing where the actual line is. We could see men far off in China loading a little boat on the river, and hear the geese and chickens and water buffaloes from far away. It was warmish, gray cloudy, soft. Went back on

Hong Kong side-street scene.

the train to Kowloon (nine dragons) where our ship was—the seamen out handling rigging, sheaves and cables. Joanne is wearing her fine yellow raincoat. The villages in mainland Hong Kong have a very different feeling from those in Japan. The rows in the gardens aren't so straight, the buildings not so neat—and the building material is brick instead of wood (though roofs are thatch); the people all wear the wide trousers and jackets, men and women alike, and the coolie hats in the field. But Hong Kong has food in a way no Japanese town could. The Japanese simply don't have the Chinese sense for cooking and eating (and a Japanese meal out, dinner party, say, is always a drag until people are finally drunk enough on sake to loosen up; whereas the Chinese have glorious multi-course banquets as a matter of course). In Hong Kong it's like walking along the market sections of Grant Avenue, Chinatown, only better, the wineshops and herb shops in between. That evening to an Australian-run bar for a while, then back to the end of the pier, looking across to the Victoria (Island) side, the celebrated lights going up the steep hill, drinking beer in the dark—a freighter comes in, blotting out the neon, the bridge decks alight, and a junk in full sail, batwing taut membrane over bones—goes out darkly and silent, a single yellow kerosene lamp dim in the stern.

The houses on the New Territory are all thatched, dry brown colors as the parched winter brown of the long plain stretching north—fallow paddies, with water buffalo, cows, pigs, and flocks of geese here and there browsing.

The dried out winter ricefields
men far off loading junks in the river
bales of rice on their shoulders
a little boat poles out
   —roosters and geese—
    —looking at China

Bought $347 worth of rupees in Hong Kong at 7 Rs to $1 U.S., where official rate in India is 4.75 to $1. Ship sailed at midnight and we were bound for Saigon.

Out of Hong Kong they moved Joanne and me from our cabin-class cabins and put us together in one tiny two-man cabin in the tourist-class section. Food was still to be taken deck-class, but our living quarters had been altered. I never understood why except they did get a large number of additional cabin-class passengers, Indians and Chinese, and perhaps were overcrowded. So now in the messhall, besides our previous friends, there were ladies in saris and pigtailed old Chinese ladies in silk trousers—and the waters were warm, we were sunbathing on deck. At night took up the star map and a flashlight, and identified the southern stars, Canopus and Acher-nar, and the Southern Cross, until one of the seamen came down from the bridge and said our little flashing of the flashlight was hard on the bridge lookout, so we stopped. Always in motion.

Looking at the PRC.

Coasting South Vietnam—come into muddy waters, the smell from ashore—go in a bay and up the river. Both banks jungle swamps, a bird or a fishing canoe now and then. A thick almost-comfortable warmth over it all. Turns and twists in the river. A freighter comes sailing over the jungle. One P.M. land in Saigon—surrounded by shaggy ricefield delta plains, a few thatched houses in clumps of palm. Long bridge and double-spire church visible . . . Saigon is really French. They sell French bread everywhere, right along with funny-looking broiled animal innards, fruits and kinds of fish and vegetables which knowing the name wouldn't help you. The women are all beautiful and wear silk pajamas with a silk tunic and long loose hair, and apparently brassieres that make them all come to sharp points in front. Walked a bit in the afternoon, and then out in the night street stalls—fruit juices, caged birds, crushed sugarcane with ice and lime. Next day went to the botanical gardens and zoo and museum compound, dug most of all the gibbon which has no tail and a maniac laugh while running on the ground with his arms, which are longer than his whole body, sort of crossed behind his neck. Tall trees, shuttered, colored houses, white or yellow walls. The architecture seems to be colonial Franco-Spanish. We feel the elephant's trunk nose finger some apples from the ship. Then she curtseyed.

Vietnam women fluttering and trailing high collared, tight-waisted, loose floppy ankles and thin silk swish legs—high small sharp breasts, waves of black heavy clean hair. Always a gold ring in the right ear. Sidewalk cafes and cheap beer, so later in

Gary Snyder in Saigon.

the day we sit and watch, eat ham sandwich and French pastries. Sail back down the river at 1:30 in the afternoon. You'd never guess there was any kind of war going on around here, but for a very rare truck going through with soldiers in jungle outfits, but no weapons visible, no guards with submachine guns on the corners or guys in tanks parked at intersections. Yet we read in the newspapers of ambushes and kidnappings just 15 miles out of town. Government of South Vietnam is bunch of Catholic elite westernized prudes anyhow, completely out of touch with "the people."

Next was Singapore. As we approached it the weather became muggy and the ocean surface heavy and oily, the water changed from blue to green. Also I got dysentery about then, terrible cramps. So I went ashore for only five hours in Singapore, feeling miserable, and remember little from that time. Our new passengers included a lot of adolescent Sikh boys with their fuzzed young faces and girlish wisps of hair sticking out from under their turbans. Indian women and children all over the deck, squabbling—and a tall white-haired fine-featured Swiss lady with her Chinese husband. They had just recently left mainland China—had been traders in Shanghai for many many years. With them was their son who looked in his mid-twenties. They were on their way to Switzerland. They claimed no good had come out of communism in China; the peasants were worse off than before on account of bad agricultural practices, everyone miserable and resigned—no bars or lights at night, everybody the same dull clothes, blue suit; but they were freely allowed to leave China and were

Saigon Public Market.

never in any way molested. I think they just found life getting dull there, and they had no love for Chiang Kai-shek.

Now we were crossing the Bay of Bengal, bound for Ceylon. The Indians out on the deck all day listening to Indian radio on their Singapore or Hong Kong transistors. Saris blowing and swirling about the deck—several hours spent reexamining our loads and lightening our packs—give away the long underwear (which was scratchy old army surplus stuff full of holes anyhow)—and Joanne planning to leave her heavy coat and high heels behind in Colombo to pick up later—even so we have about 40 lbs. each, with sleeping bags, cooking pots, etc. We knew the jig was up when I went up on deck and saw our two Ceylonese teacher friends had mysteriously changed from Western dress and were now in Ceylonese sarongs—and weren't bothering to speak much English any more—they were in their own waters. That night we passed the light on the southern end of Ceylon, and at dawn we were in Colombo harbor, to be thrust off the security of the ship and into the "world."

II. Ceylon: Colombo & Kandy

CEYLON—TAPROBANE, in old books. Shakespeare calls it that, I believe. Or was it Milton. Carried on trade with the Roman Empire—the old port is now called Galle—

Chess on board the Cambodge,
Mr. Abeyewardena.

famous for its precious stones and spices and elephants, even then—Portuguese left a big mark here—many Ceylonese families named Da Silva and Perera, although their features show no trace of Western blood, now—and they are mostly Hinayana Buddhists; the others are Roman Catholic or (the Tamil-speaking people) Hindu.

Our ship anchored a dab offshore in Colombo, so we rode in on a launch—pitching sharply, a windy day, and went easily through customs. Outside the customs shed is the tourist information bureau, which though nice to look at was staffed by one lazy sexy-looking girl who wasn't much help to us. They know our sort of tourist (rucksack) and know we don't bring in much dollar. (In India it was different, though.) Claude Dalenberg had given us a lead on a place to stay, so we went to the British Soldiers' and Seaman's Institute next door to the YMCA, which sure enough had rooms to rent. Cement floors and all, the big punka fan on the ceiling lazily spinning with the speed adjuster set on the wall by the light switch. This was the pattern we had on all rooms—two cots, a punka, a table. We stretched out a clothesline and rolled out our bedding—to sleep on top of, it was too hot to get into anything, and went out to look for food. Since the country was in the grip of a strike at that time, and the city gas was on strike, restaurants had almost no food. We ate bananas and meat rolls. I got a haircut at the YMCA, and the punka fan blew the cut hair all over the place, into eyes and down my neck—the barber didn't even seem to notice it. I had him shave off my beard (Joanne wanted to see me without it)—and when I got

Messageries Maritime
ship Cambodge.
At dock in Colombo.

back to the room she would scarcely let me in the door, claiming she didn't know me. It was a shock to see my face without hair. So I let it grow right back again. A beard is a good thing to have in India anyhow, as it turned out. We bought some Ceylon rupees from a jeweler at the fine rate of eight to one dollar, had dinner in a Chinese restaurant which was the poorest Chinese food I've ever seen—but relatively cheap. Back at the B.S.S.I. observed the inhabitants drinking beer on the first floor, a Ceylonese brand called Nuwara Eliya. We had one too—they really were seamen, or international tramp tourists of the sort we saw so many of, beards and rucksacks, wearing boots or sandals—usually German or Swedish or Australian.

Beggar kids waiting for us outside the door, and this is a cheap place, 6 rupees a night for the two of us. Less than fifty cents each. Women next door carrying metal pans of broken concrete on their heads, black as Africans, wearing dusty purple saris. A construction project.

In the evening walked through Pettah, a native quarter—heh heh of pilots (guys that want to show you stores), beggars and merchants. Men wearing sarongs, with wide leather or web belts, usually barefoot. Dark skin and hairy ears. In the Pettah unrecognizable fruits and vegetables piled up. Cools off in the evening. Eat more bananas and go to bed.

Next day figured out bus and went to the Dehiwala zoo five miles south of Colombo. Fine elephants and many animals of all sorts—supposed to be the best zoo in the

Abeyewardena family,
near Colombo.

east—but we didn't like all the cages, especially the leopards looked unhappy. It's funny to see monkeys in cages and other monkeys playing around outside of cages. Visited a Buddhist temple in the afternoon, Dipaduttamaramaya vihara, built 150 years ago by the king of Thailand. Gaudy colors and lackadaisical cleanliness which is just the opposite of most Japanese Buddhist temples, but at least the *people* here are Buddhists, where in Japan the only Buddhists, virtually, are the Buddhist priests. We met the head Bhikku, who spoke English and is trying to raise money for a trip to America. He has just finished building a big library full of Sinhalese, Pali, and English-language Buddhist literature. But I thought these Bhikkus are arrogant and lazy.

Next day, 30 December. Followed up on the invitation of one of the Ceylonese schoolteachers who was on the *Cambodge* to visit him. Took a fifty-minute bus ride into the countryside—lush, full of banana and coconut trees, and little palm-leaf, thatch huts along the roadside, barefoot people strolling about. Get off in front of a school surrounded by palm trees. Dharmapala Vidyalaya school—our friend Mr. Abeyewardena is principal. A fellow from the school leads us to his house, which is red-tile roofed with mud walls. He is a very well-known man in Ceylon, it turns out, and his school is quite famous, as a Buddhist private-preparatory or high school, coeducational. He is not wealthy by any Western standard but I suppose in Ceylon or India he would represent the upper middle class. He was educated in London School of Economics and is a most literate man. He has a well-educated wife, three charming

Bullock cart in Colombo.

daughters, one small son, and one seventeen-year-old son who is apparently not too bright, although not exactly a "deficient." The middle daughter, about twelve, is a chess fiend and he says she is pretty good (he ought to know because he whipped me on the ship every time we played). They have a couple maids in the kitchen, women wearing the dark blue or maroon saris which are the standard wear of lower caste women. The fire is wood, the pots are brass or earthenware set on brick tripods. They are juicing the white out of coconuts on a kind of shredder-knife, and putting it into a curry sauce (coconut is used in all sorts of cooking). Then they give us a special kind of green coconut milk to drink, and a "custard apple" fruit to eat, which is a bumpy-looking red-skinned thing with a soft white flesh which tastes just like custard.

Everybody calls bananas "plantains" here. Mangoes, they said, were out of season. We ate some jaggery candy, made from sap of a palm.

So we had a nice curry dinner with them—although it was a little strange, because Mr. Abeyewardena had to leave suddenly when two men came on some kind of urgent national educational business, and his wife and daughters served us, but wouldn't eat *with* us (the custom). Then we chatted a long time after dinner, and they made us up a bed on the floor. Next morning we were planning to leave Colombo and pass on, inland, to Kandy. Thundershowers in the night and swordfight-rattling of the big palm leaves whipping about in the wind.

So we got up at 5 A.M. From Mr. Abe's house, took the bus back to town, picked

Right: Kandy. Gary on an elephant.

Opposite page: Kandy, the "Temple of the Tooth."

up our rucksacks, and caught the train (walking all the way to the station) for Kandy, the old capital of Ceylon and sort of the Buddhist center. Train climbed a bit, after the first fifty miles. Landscape of coconut palm groves and ricefields. At trainstops men sell coconuts for drinking instead of soda pop—buy one and they swiftly cut a square out of the top with a knife, and you drink directly from the shell. Then the train began to climb, and we saw some really splendid scenery of jungled steep hills, some with rocky cliffs, great forests, steeply terraced ricefields, and clouds floating amongst it all. Also passed through areas of commercial tea plantations, hillsides covered with low clipped tea bushes (looking rather similar to Japanese tea-growing lands). Kandy is about 1000 feet above sea level.

Our plan was to stay in the youth hostel here, which it turned out was one cement room with two beds within the Boy Scout headquarters building. We had a hard time even finding that. Once in, strung up our clothesline (Joanne was always rinsing things out first thing we got someplace), took a bath (they had showers here) and then went out, running into Helmut the German boy from the *Cambodge,* who had also gotten off in Colombo. We went with him and a Ceylonese fellow he'd met to see the elephants get washed in some river. This was a nice ten-minute bus ride. At the river the mahouts very friendly, urged us to ride an elephant, sit on its right knee, etc., which we smilingly did, and were then asked for two rupees. We soon discovered you don't get nothing for sheer friendliness in these parts. Afternoon later went to the Temple

of the Tooth—Dadala Madigawa—a very nice-looking white stone structure with a tile roof, handsome woodworking inside . . . the most celebrated Buddhist shrine in Ceylon. It enshrines a tooth of the Buddha, so they say. The Portuguese claim they looted the temple three centuries ago, took the tooth out and threw it away. The Buddhists claim that all they got was a fake tooth. I saw a plaster cast of the tooth enshrined at Kandy, and it was about two inches long and looked wicked. They must have made the Buddhas bigger and fiercer in them days.

At 5 P.M. I was inside the temple, shoes off and waiting with the worshipers to go past the casket of the tooth (the real thing itelf is shown once a year). After half an hour of drum beating and blowing on trumpets by men with sarongs and bare chests (looking and sounding like a Hollywood spectakl) we filed in, around, and through—several hundred Ceylonese and me—and saw this big jewel-encrusted casket on jewel-encrusted cushions and half hid by drapes, while big fat Bhikkus raked in flower and money offerings.

Walked back, stopping at the Silverdale Hotel for dinner—ordering a curry dinner and getting plate after plate of various curries, soups, curds (i.e. yogurt), crackers, sliced vegetables, so that Joanne started croaking doom and saying they had misunderstood what we'd ordered and would shortly be charging us a huge sum of money. When the bill came, it was exactly what we'd thought—at the beginning—about 22 cents. But so hot, our faces were bright red and tears streaming down our cheeks by

Right: German Bhikku,
Nyanaponika Thero.

Opposite page, left: Sri Lanka.
Countryside near Colombo.

Opposite page, right: Anuradhapura Stupa.

the end of the meal. This was New Year's Eve, but we couldn't even find a place to buy likker, and didn't know nobody, so walked on home to the Boy Scout headquarters, to the sound of people drumming everywhere, in their houses (I never did find out just what the drumming was about), and fell asleep listening to the transistor radio from Japan (Joanne had received as a going-away present from her National Electric Co. class).

On the first of January 1962 took the bus a few miles and saw the finest botanical garden in the East, one of the finest tropical botanical gardens anywhere—Peradeniya. They have every possible tropical tree and bamboo here, from all the Indies, South and Central America, Southeast Asia, Africa. Was started about a hundred years ago by the English. Long avenues of talipot, cabbage, and palmyra palms. Various aerial-root type trees, forming whole structures full of bats or monkeys, and some giant bamboo groves. Took us several hours to walk through it all. Afternoon went back to Kandy and climbed up into the jungle hills of the Temple of the Tooth to look for the hut of a German monk, Nyanaponika Thera, we'd heard about. Walked various trails, watched wild monkeys, and discovered our ankles covered with leeches several times. Eventually located the Bhikku's place, called "Forest Hermitage"—I had read a few of his pamphlets long ago. He is a sweet elderly fellow in his yellow robes with freckled skin and looks like he might sunburn too easily for this climate. We spent the afternoon til it began to grow dark talking in his neat little cottage.

He put leech medicine on our bleeding ankles. He has just finished a book for Rider & Co. (London) called *The Heart of Buddhist Meditation*—based on the Hinayana meditation on "mindfulness" called Satipatthana. He had studied meditation for a while in Burma.

III. *Anuradhapura*

NEXT DAY BY BUS north out of Kandy, down to the plains, stopping at a town with a Buddhist cave on the hill (Dambulla) and again north—our rucksacks up on the top of the bus, ladder up the back—to Anuradhapura. Into the dryer northwest section of Ceylon. Anuradhapura was one of the world's great cities, between second century B.C. and eleventh century A.D. The dry part of Ceylon was watered by an elaborate system of canals and reservoirs in those days, and the city was ten miles or so across, capital of the Singhalese kings. Combination of silting in the canals (from overcutting the hill jungles around Kandy?) and invasions of Tamil-speaking people from south India, the Pandyan Kingdom, drove the Singhalese back from the plains into the hills, which are wet enough, but also very unhealthy. The population reverted somewhat, and went down in number, so that the people the Portuguese saw were but a fragment of what had been a great civilization. Ceylon still doesn't have the

Right: Anuradhapura Stupa.

Opposite page, left: Fellow traveller from Japan Helmut Kugl and Gary. In Kandy.

Opposite page, right: Sri Lankan country scene.

population it had at its height. They are just now trying to figure out how to put the canal and reservoir system back into use.

So, at Anuradhapura we found a Buddhist pilgrims' place to stay, and walked out; the biggest thing to be seen an enormous white stupa, over two hundred feet high, and lesser stupas here and there, with foundations and stone railings or posts scattered everywhere, remains of great buildings. All in white granite. Some of these with fragmentary carving on them, which we did rubbings and photographs of. Acres of close-cropped clean grasses, big trees, half-tame monkeys. Next to the site is a large, large pond, fringed with lovely trees. A few pious Buddhists circumambulating the stupas. One of the stupas said to contain "the left collarbone of Lord Buddha." Almost a mile to the town proper, where meals are to be bought . . . Anuradhapura site is under the Archeological Survey, and all shops and businesses have been cleared out of it.

From Anuradhapura an all night train ride to Talaimannar, the ferry-port for India. Arriving at dawn. A stiff wind out, and nothing but a long golden sandy beach and palm trees to be seen, and the pier stretching out into the water. It took hours to go through customs (the immigration officer, a big stocky fellow in shorts, looking at the form I filled in "occupation *writer*" asks me "You a journalist? Going to write articles about India?" To which I laugh and say, "What's the matter, you afraid that somebody write something about India?" but he was serious, and even though I told

him I was a poet held up on stamping my passport for half an hour. I know he could not have refused us entrance, though, especially if I'd bitch).

Fine white sand . . . yellow-green choppy waves—lighthouse—warm wind. Across the waters, and into the opposite port of Dhanushkodi, a few shacks on a sandspit, and a customs shed. It was nightfall when we were cleared through (having safely smuggled our 2500 rupees) and the train came, backed out onto the sandspit, and a wild mob of people started fighting into it, climbing through windows, etc. I don't know how we managed to get in. There, in the back of one of the third-class compartments, we found a white woman stretched out on a bench, who turned out to be an American missionary, and she sat up and shared her seat with Joanne. She was an Assembly of God type who had been in the field of India since 1937, a small village in the South. She spoke fluent Tamil. Said she'd lost two husbands in the mission work, the second one just last summer. I said Assembly of God is Pentecostal, isn't it? She says, yes, but not like some of the Pentecostals you've heard about.

IV. South India

AT 2 A.M. we got off the train in the town of Madurai, our first real place in India. Got into a railway retiring room (most stations have four or five rooms with baths to rent for about 5 rupees per 24 hours) and washed up, washed some clothes, and slept until dawn. We'd stopped in this town to see the Hindu temple of Minakshi, so off we walked in search of it. Not hard to find, as it had four towers close to 200 feet high, one in the middle of each wall. South India, people half-naked and barefoot, all talking Tamil or some other Dravidian language, palm trees everywhere, and cheap fruit, especially bananas. Minakshi temple is a temple to the wife of Shiva . . . enormous, must cover close to fifty acres. Walls within walls, the sanctuary at the center. "Madurai means SWEETNESS" . . . was capital of the Pandyans . . . "Strabo states that a Pandya King sent an Ambassador in B.C. 27 to the court of Augustus Caesar . . ." We must leave our sandals at the entrance of the temple outer wall, pass through a *gopuram* (tower) gate and past stalls of sandalwood-image sellers, devotional color prints, . . . the walls and posts covered with stone carvings of girls, elephants, trees, vines, lions, snakes, and more girls. Joanne and I wandered and wandered, in and in farther, until we found ourselves in a procession going into the sanctum of Shiva wife Minakshi ("The fish-eyed one") . . . and were chased out by some indignant temple official. Somewhere sound of drums and trumpets, and rolling clouds of incense, such rich smell, the people with red dots and three ash streaks on their foreheads. Piety and devotion.

In the religious picture stalls they sell bright color prints of Shiva, Buddha (looking like a woman), Christ (holding his chest open showing a great drippy bleeding heart

Madurai, the Minakshi Temple.

within) and Gandhi, with a halo. Shiva is by far the most attractive, with his purple skin, a snake coiled around his neck and another cobra on his outstretched arm, long hair coiled up on his head, sitting in meditation posture with glorious Himalayan backdrop behind.

From a piece of temple literature:

"Then one enters the Minakshi shrine. In the eastern inner prakara can be seen the statues of Tirumal Naik and his two wives. The Goddess Minakshi in the Sanctum Sanctorum is of enchanting beauty and grace. To the north of this shrine is the separate shrine of Lord Sundareswara. The garbagriha is called Ashtagiri Vimana which is supported by eight elephants on the four sides. In front of this shrine is the gold plated Dwajasthamba (flag staff) in what is called the Kambathadi Mantapa. In the pillars round the flag-post there are sculptural figures representing the wedding of Minakshi and Sundareswara, Gajananamurthi, Tripurantakamurthi, Dakshinamurthi, Ardhanariswara, Nataraja, Parvathi, Parameswara on the Rishpa (bull) and Kailas with Ravana. . . . Just inside the northern tower there are five music pillars of single stone with 22 sub-pillars each. Playing on these small pillars one can hear different musical sounds."

V. Pondicherry

THAT EVENING caught a third-class sleeping car on northbound for Pondicherry. Third-class sleeping means cars with huge ledges overhead, and a ledge that folds up and hooks on chains where the back was, above the usual bench seat, making in all a triple-tiered bunk arrangement for each seat. Luggage goes under the bottom seat or just on the aisle between the two facing benches (compartment style). We got into one of these and slept in our board bunks, like Chinamen being sent back to China to die, until early morning, transferred to another train, and by 7 A.M. were nearing the coast.

Train we transferred to was a small, deserted local engine, and when we climbed into the third-class car it looked like the compartment I got into was empty. Actually a couple of people were huddled across from us, under a big handspun shawl. I started to put my rucksack under the seat, and found a man sleeping there, so put it on the seat beside me. Joanne huddled up and slept some more, while I watched the pair across from us. They stirred and moved around some; it was a man with long hair, earrings, and a girl about twelve . . . when they threw back the shawl I saw both were dressed only in skimpy loincloths under the single shawl . . . she had large gold hoops in her ears, bangles on her wrists and ankles, and wild brownish hair down over her shoulders, looked as if it had never been combed . . . both were barefoot, and

Opposite page and right:
Pondicherry Ashram.

covered with dust, looked at Joanne and me with kind of vague wild curiosity . . . at the next stop they both got off on the wrong side of the train and walked off across the tracks and into a grove . . . They had been riding free, and were (as I came to know later) probably "tribal people," still thinking of themselves as members of a certain tribe, not necessarily Hindus, in fact still living rather primitive lives . . . they both had lovely faces.

Pondicherry was formerly a French enclave and when we got there, sure enough the policemen and train officials were speaking French. We took a bicycle rickshaw to the head office of the Sri Aurobindo Ashram where we planned to stay. An ashram is a unique Indian institution, it is a religious community based around some teacher and branch of Hinduism; the person of the teacher being very important. Not all ashrams are actually religious—the Gandhi ashrams and Vinoba Bhave ashrams are primarily aimed at combining a kind of spiritual communism with community service and social work. The Aurobindo ashram was founded sometime after world war I (I think) by Sri Aurobindo Ghose, a Bengali who had been educated from childhood on in England, returned to India and became a rabid nationalist, and then switched to yoga. He claimed to have founded a new type of yoga, "Integral Yoga," and heralded a new "Divine Life" on earth. From the mid-twenties on he was assisted in his work by a woman known only as The Mother. I have been told she was a French lady to begin with, who left her husband to live in Pondicherry. She came gradually to be the person actually running the ashram, and Sri Aurobindo spent the last some years of his life in virtual seclusion. He died in 1950. The Mother runs it all now. I had heard of Aurobindo some years ago around the Academy of Asian Studies. Frederick Spiegelberg was an Aurobindo fan, and they had a few copies of Aurobindo's huge book *The Life Divine* around. I don't want to go into his philosophy here, but it is a rather eclectic spirit-oriented system which has affinities with neo-Platonism, Gnosticism, as well as Vedanta, and it is not truly monistic, as Vedanta is, but rather belongs, it seems to me, in the class with antimatter dualisms like Manichaeism, Nestorian Xtianity, some sorts of Gnosticism, and Catharites. I rather doubt that it is a truly Indian philosophy. Maybe if I read more on it I'll change my mind.

The ashram is considered to be the best organized in India. It has supposedly 1300 members, all under the direct control of The Mother. They live in various buildings and houses owned by the ashram (i.e., owned by The Mother) scattered through the old French section of Pondicherry. ". . . a few things are strictly forbidden: they are— (1) politics, (2) smoking, (3) alcoholic drink and (4) sex enjoyment"—this applies only to actual inmates of the ashram, not guests (thank god!).

Now the funny thing is, to digress, that this absurd list of prohibitions, once you are within India, seems less and less outrageous. The prohibition of politics is probably the one that would hurt most Indians most. But the rest of us might give up politics. As for smoking, Indian tobacco was so bad I quit smoking in India anyway, and haven't taken it up again yet. Alcohol is almost impossible to buy in India, rather expensive if you find it, and absolutely foul to drink. Actually illegal in many states. As for "sex enjoyment" (and they mean this to apply to married inmates of the ashram along with everyone else), practically all Indian semireligious or religious traditional thought is in agreement on the notion that sexual activity of any sort is deleterious to Spiritual Progress. Brahmacharya is considered a very Good Thing. One who practices continence, usually a married man who has taken a vow of continence, is called a Brahmacharin. Gandhi was a Brahmacharin, from something like 1914 on never slept with his wife, and urged all his followers to adopt similar practice. Somebody once taxed Gandhi with this saying, "you became a Brahmacharin after you were all dried up anyway"—to which he replied, "my wife never looked so attractive to me, nor was my sexual potency ever as strong, as when I took the vow." Of course, a family man isn't supposed to do this until he's at least had a son.

The only exception to this view in religious circles is amongst the Shaivite-Shakti-Tantric circles (which people say still flourish in Orissa and Bengal) where sexual intercourse is practiced as a ritual designed, after long preparation, to hook everyday orgasm into the Cosmic Orgasm. But nobody (except the millions of peasants and untouchables) takes sex simply as sex, and leaves it at that. Anyway, anything that Gandhi urged is tantamount to an *order* to the semi-intelligentsia (except get along with Muslims).

To get back to Pondicherry, it is a lovely French-looking town, deserted almost—really dead but for the ashram, facing on a long white beach, with warm gentle surf. On side alleys you notice the bristly long-snouted black pigs rooting about, eating horrible garbage, and the hovels of the Scheduled Castes (i.e., untouchables) which make up a major portion of the population of South India.

Two little girls squatting on the cement rim of a canal, stark naked, taking craps, talking to each other all the while, the yellow shit sort of dribbling down the edge of the cement, then up they jump and run off playing.

Secretary at the ashram headquarters sent us in a bike rick to a place called Parc-a-charbon, right by the sea, where we were to stay a few nights. We got a little room with two wooden cots, actually sort of boxes with drawers underneath to put your gear in, and hasps for padlocking, a thin mattress on top, and a wood frame over it with a mosquito netting. A table, a chair, a big earthenware waterpot in the corner, damp all over, the water inside cool from the constant evaporation.

We were the only people living here but for a Cambodian Buddhist monk, some lay Yogins, and the man who was caretaker for the building (a converted godown from French merchant days) who was a large goodnatured fellow with elephantiasis of one leg and hence had smelly wet bandages wrapped around it all the time and couldn't go far because it was so hard to walk. His room was covered with pictures of The Mother.

We got to see The Mother the next morning early, at her *darshan*. *Darshan* is

Joanne and Gary at Pondicherry.

another big Indian thing, it simply means appearance, or presence. Underlying it is a belief that you don't need to be instructed or led by a holy person, just by proximity or seeing them you are immeasurably benefited. So The Mother appears every morning about 6:15 A.M. on the balcony of her house, and three or four hundred people gather on the street below. She comes out, looks at everybody slowly in big circles, then looks up and out and goes into "a meditative trance"—eyes open, body shifting from time to time. Then, smiling a bit, she looks at everybody once more, and backs off the balcony. She has a gauzy silk scarf over her head and brow, and a kind of twenties-ish elegance. A real production. And she must be close to her eighties. Her age doesn't seem to worry the ashram people, though.

A woman from Canada named Beverly Siegerman, who has been at the ashram three years, told us that The Mother would never die, and that by a gradual process of physical-spiritual transformation some of the other people around the ashram would live forever too. The goal is that mankind becomes, in time, entirely transmuted, lives immortally and sexlessly.

Some of the people there are quite intelligent, but for their acceptance of some of these doctrines. That's India for you. There is a staggering amount of Aurobindo literature in English, all published right in Pondicherry by ashram workers. The POINT is, though, from my standpoint, that there was no practice of any kind—study, meditation, etc., to be seen. And this is what I am always looking for. No matter how ridiculous a theory or doctrine may be, it may have associated meditation exercises which are pragmatically quite good. Aurobindo ashramites seem to exist entirely on a devotion-and-faith basis, "open yourself to the influence of The Mother." This also can be a valid path (i.e., devotion and submission) but it requires a very critical study of doctrine.

VI. Tiruvannamalai

WE STAYED FIVE DAYS in Pondicherry, mostly because the food was healthy, the ocean breezes pleasant, and it gave us a good chance to wash clothes, get our bearings, and ask various people questions about India. Before daybreak on January 11 we caught a rickety bus, rucksacks on top, for the inland town of Tiruvannamalai.

—small figures in the dawn squat in dry riverbeds.
—a mysterious gob of carrion flew into the bus and caught on a window-rail.
—surf rolling up on the Pondicherry sands, "white town" and "black town" canoes in breakers, netting fish a few minutes walk from the "perfect society" the squalor and mud huts, dark people little girls naked but for a shiny metal triangle hung over the vulva, on a string. Nose-holes, three or four ear-holes, even little babies wear jewelry.

Black pigs wallowing and rummaging. They look the best adjusted.
—gray hairy water buffaloes with swept-back horns and low-slung ears.
    White frill-necked Brahman bulls.
Bougainvillea flowers.

By noon we were in Tiruvannamalai, headquarters of another ashram, the Sri Ramana Maharshi Ashram. This is a stony landscape, the town dominated by a high barren hill behind, Arunachala—sacred to Shiva. A very large Hindu temple is at the foot of the hill, with its many *gopuram* towers. Around to the south, also at the foot of this hill, is the Maharshi's ashram. Here we were met by an Englishman, Arthur Osborne, and his Czech wife. Osborne and his wife have a house hard by the ashram. He is an Oxford-educated philosophically bent man in his fifties or sixties, who has been in India since before the war. Came out as a "seeker." Ramana Maharshi, who has been dead since the early fifties, was the man Osborne hit on, and became the biographer of. He has several books out, mostly published by Rider & Co., not only on Maharshi but on Hinduism and Indian history.

Ramana Maharshi was a genuine Jnana-yogin (adept of wisdom-yoga, as compared with devotional-yoga) who became totally enlightened without any great effort while still a young man. He went up on Arunachala mountain and lived in a cave by a spring for many years, then a few of his followers built an ashram for him at the foot of the hill.

He was apparently a very sweet person, talking very little and having almost no teaching method or even interest in teaching. He had a pet cow named Lakshmi, he shaved his head and beard once every forty days, never wore anything but a loincloth, and spent much of this time in blissful trance. He knew no English. His one approach was to tell everyone to ask the question "Who?" of themselves. Who feels? Who thinks? Who suffers? Who wants salvation? Who asks who? People who are existentially bugged and meditate steadily on this "Who?" for a while are bound to get some insights. I believe it myself—in fact Maharshi is the closest to Zen method of any Hindu yoga.

Once, the story goes, a cobra came into the stone hall where Ramana spent his later days and slithered right over his legs. On being asked how he had felt, after the cobra went away, he replied in one word: "cool."

The Osbornes put us up in a little room on top of their house, from which we could look about the landscape, and through a mass of bougainvillea up toward Arunachala. We had our lunches at the ashram dining hall, sitting crosslegged on the stone floor, putting a platter of a few leaves stitched together with fiber before us on the floor. A server came along and put rice on the platter, then another fellow came and poured some curry sauce and some ghee on the rice, and put a brass cup of water down. This we ate with our right hands. Afterwards the leaf platter is thrown away, and one washes his hand at a faucet outside. After the meal, coffee is served in a brass cup. South Indians always drink coffee, mixed with milk and lots of sugar, and poured back and forth between two brass pots until it gets frothy. The south Indian curries are very hot, but never actually inedible, and in a way rather fun. The dining hall had about thirty people eating, loincloth-dressed sadhus with long hair, layman-type ashramites with white dhoti or sari, and a Swiss lady in white sari. Many old pictures of Ramana Maharshi on the walls, including one giant portrait of him standing by his cow Lakshmi. Since Maharshi is no longer there, it is the aura of his previous presence which brings people here, or as the Ashram pamphlet described it—"Saturated with the Benign Presence of Sri Maharshi the Ashram confers the unequalled blessing of peace, bliss, and happiness to the devotee, whatsoever the religion he may profess. Many devotees gather morning and evening in the old hall and in front of the Samadhi (tomb) for silent meditation and prayer . . ."

Also in the afternoon a bunch of little Brahman boys get Veda-chanting practice, which we went to hear, and it was indeed moving to hear the melodic syllables of the Vedas even from these little kids. Sanskrit is a magical language.

Osborne had a lot of interesting old-India-hand holy-man-circuit gossip. Next day Joanne and I climbed up to the cave where Maharshi had lived 25 years, and got a good view out over the South India landscape—long rocky plains with great boulders lying on them, occasional watered villages with palm groves, little paddy fields with peasants irrigating from deep tanks or wells by ox-pull bucket and pulley arrangements, and to the west, the fantastically jagged shapes of the Eastern Ghats

Opposite: Joanne Kyger, at Arthur Osborne's house.
Sacred Mountain Arunachala behind.

(I think that's what they were). The land there is pretty dry and rocky—the monsoon waters it, and water is caught in artificial ponds.

All around Tiruvannamalai are remains of ancient reservoirs and building foundations. Like so much of India, past glory was greater. We went that afternoon on a *pradakshina,* or holy circumambulation, around Arunachala. Whenever you circumambulate something (in Buddhism, a stupa, a chorten, a pagoda, or a meditation hall, also a mountain), it is always done clockwise, keeping the object on your right. Good thing to know. Anyhow Mrs. Osborne assured us that the merit of circumambulation would be enhanced immensely if we went barefoot. So we did, all seven miles of it, mostly on gravel and asphalt road. My feet didn't begin to feel sore until the last mile, and Joanne's didn't hurt her at all.

Mrs. Osborne wore white sari, and was constantly being greeted by peasant women along the way. She speaks very good Tamil, it seems (which is rare—everyone says Tamil is terribly difficult, and few foreigners know it, whereas everyone in northern India who's been there a year or so can speak Hindi). She was great friends with peasants because she is a homeopathic medicine expert and gives treatments free. Homeopathic medicine, which is pretty much in line with the old Ayurvedic medicine, is very popular in India, among educated folks too.

Cows begin to creep up on you here. Like the ashram pamphlet says—"The resonant chant of the Vedas by the pupils and the gentle looks of the cows of several breeds enchant the visitor, Indian and other." And as for Lakshmi (who in real life is the wife of Vishnu), they say "she was unusually attached to Sri Bhagavan, and . . . attained liberation by Sri Bhagavan's (i.e. Lord Maharshi's) Special Grace at the time of her death." They are, when well kept, the most beautiful cows in the world. Even Marco Polo remarked on this in his Travels, speaking of the oxen of Rudnabar, which were white Brahmans, "They are the loveliest things in the world to look at."

I don't quote all this to make fun of Maharshi's place, because it had the nicest feeling of any ashram in South India, and was one of our pleasantest stops. Disciples are never up to the masters, in these situations.

We were moving on something of a schedule, and couldn't stay longer there, so at 4:30 next morning we were up, caught a tonga (horse-wagon) into the bus station (which is a shit-strewn field) and were off for the city of Madras. A six-hour ride, through arid plains and fields of dry brush, trees and rocks, except for the few irrigated paddies.

    Palm fringing stonefield
      crows   and a white bird circle

VII. Madras

THE INSTANT we got off the bus in Madras we were hit by one of those common-in-India circumstances that can drive you frantic: an enormous press of bicycle-rickshaw drivers all insisting you ride with them; and you know that none of them can be trusted to give you an honest price or even a direct ride to where you want to go. They were so numerous and quarrelsome that after a few minutes we shouldered our packs in disgust and decided to walk to the main railway station—which I knew couldn't be far. Asking a few people on the way we located it and took a retiring room, then set out to find the tourist bureau to get some maps, pamphlets, and information. After considerable searching (the street-numbering system worked on principles I couldn't grasp) found it—and it was closed. So we fell into a bookstore, picked up a few pamphlets, and noticed a copy of Kerouac's *Scripture of the Golden Eternity* in the Hinduism section, and later Joanne found a copy of *Howl* (City Lights edition) in the art section. It was one of the three or four best bookstores we saw in India, as it turned out later. There are lots of fine books on Indian history, art, and anthropology published in India, sold cheap, and never distributed outside the country. I picked up a few from time to time.

Madras is a nicely aspected town, clean by Indian standards, modern, and quite progressive. Many people in the Madras area speak English—considerably more than in the northern Hindi-speaking regions. The reason is that Tamil, Telugu, and Kannada are such difficult and exotic languages that from some time ago English became the second language of all semi-educated or educated south Indians, not only for purposes of communicating with the British, but for talking to people from Bengal, west or north India. Now that Hindi is supposed to be the official language, people in north India have quit studying English and quit using it in the various public ways they used to. The south Indians are being urged to study Hindi as a second language by the Government now, but they still feel that English is a preferable second language, i.e., more internationally useful, and are hostile to the north, "New Delhi," anyhow—the old Aryan vs. Dravidian argument, and a new southern Dravidian nationalism which is anti-Sanscritization of their south Indian culture. This is a big political issue. So it's easier for travelers in the south than the north. Another thing is, of course, that the Muslim influence was much less in the south than in the north. The temples, and traditional Hindu social customs, are less disturbed.

All the restaurants visible to the eye in Madras were vegetarian—in fact, Madras vegetarian cooking is famous all over India we later found out. So we picked out one, found a table up on the roof under the sky and surrounded by plants and people, and ordered the regular 2 rupee vegetarian dinner. We were served course after course, all we could eat of each, including two kinds of chapatties and rice, curds and banana for dessert, and a quid of betel nut each at the end. It's enough to make you become a vegetarian. A great breakfast is south Indian *masala dosa*—a sourdough tortilla-like thing, filled with vegetables—and eaten with a delicious sauce—with south Indian coffee.

The sidewalks in India seem to be covered with gobs and splashes of blood, which is betel juice. Called *pan,* it is really a mixed confection. What you get is a number of ground spices, the broken-up chunks of betel (areca) nut, and a dab of lime, all rolled up in a special kind of leaf. The whole thing is stuck in the mouth and pretty soon you start to drool red. You can swallow the juice too. It tastes like chewing on cloves and allspice, and is supposed to be good for the stomach. It has no narcotic effects, and all I can see it does is make your lips and teeth red and give your mouth a sweet spicy flavor. If it weren't so messy from all the spitting it would be a very civilized practice.

After dinner we walked back to our room and washed up, washed clothes, and ate a dozen bananas. Next morning I set out with a cookpot to buy some curds, being hungry for an Aurobindo-Ashram type breakfast—it was dark still—and after looking up and down a lot of filthy alleys found a curds-seller fresh from the country with earthenware pots full of it, and bought a quart. We made a big mixture of curds, torn up bits of bread, sliced banana, and sugar, and ate it all. Walking in those early morning dawnlight streets one must be careful, not to bump into people defecating in the gutters, or step in numerous fresh cow and human turds. Cows seem much nicer than people when it comes to shit and breath. All I wore on my feet was either Japanese zoris, or leather Indian chappals (which is like a zori pretty much) except for rare occasions when I put on high-top Japanese lug-soled hiking shoes made of nylon canvas—so one must be careful of his feet.

We had a contact in Madras, looked up and it turned out to be a young half-German half-Indian girl whose German mother ran a day school. Her name was Gita Sharma. She took us to a magnificent dance recital the next night, in celebration of the south Indian harvest festival, *pongal,* which takes place in mid-January. The dancers were two sisters about 17 who were from a well-to-do family. The recital lasted a good three hours and was really impressive. One sister was much better than the other, only in the confidence and pleasure she radiated, for both of them did identical motions throughout. Formerly dancing was the domain of the *devadasis,* temple girls, who were also "temple prostitutes," so it has been only recently that studying dance has come to be regarded as a socially acceptable study for young ladies of good family. In ancient times, around Sakyamuni's period, music-playing and dance was permissible to the well-born. Somewhere in between it lost caste.

The following day, 15 January, was *Go-puja,* cow-worship day. Cows painted in pretty colors and decorated with flowers were to be seen about. Joanne and I took the bus to Mahabalipuram this day to see the celebrated seven shrines, cave temples, and

A temple in Bhubaneswar.

shore temple, at this site—dating from the eleventh century—right on the seacoast. This place is thirty or so miles south of Madras, in a very deserted area. At one time apparently the seaport was here (Madras as a city was founded by the British, and has no natural harbor—ships anchor well offshore and everything is brought in by launch). It was hot like summer. Many fine carved reliefs illustrating Hindu myths. The complex of temple caves and shrines was inspired by the mile-long outcropping of fine white granite, so that the shrine buildings are not built out of stone, but just carved out of the living rock. A celebrated relief called "Arjuna's Penance" is here: carved on a cliff, it is 100 feet long and 40 feet high and filled with hundreds of figures and animals, including two larger-than-life size elephants.

The shore temple is a small, delicately built temple on a spit of land being eaten away by the sea. Another few hundred years, unless lots of retaining wall is built, and it may be swallowed up.

That evening went to the Agricultural Exhibit back in Madras. The American pavilion clean and good-looking, some American farm experts had figured out tools to be made of local materials by village blacksmiths good and cheap, and they were showing how to use them—a new type of harrow, and an irrigation-channel digger. Lots of new hybrid-corn species being pushed in India too, some done by back-breeding with primitive Amerindian corn. New one called "Deccan." The German pavilion was all about cows and dairying. Indian cows are lousy milk producers, it

*Orissa, Konarak
Temple main building.*

seems.—Policemen's hats are like plaid turban with sort of vane on the top. Dust crusted around the anus of a beggar-girl's show baby.—Public toilets have a picture of a man and a picture of a woman, to show sides.

VIII. *Bhubaneswar–Konarak*

ON THE SEVENTEENTH of January we caught a night train from Madras, third-class reserved bogy, bound north along the Bay of Bengal coast towards Calcutta. The seats are wood bench, so we pad them, time to stretch out and sleep. During the night stretched out on the seat and luggage rack above. Our bogy wasn't crowded at first, so that night sleeping was easy. Canteen full of halazoned water hung on a coathook by the bench. Rucksacks overhead and under the seat. Morning, we were running through barren landscape with occasional boulders and palms; rarely a paddy field or dusty little village. Hills along the western horizon all the way. Breakfast, bought at a stop, of graham flour patties called *puris* with a kind of sauce, served in a cup made of sewn leaves, and cups of boiled tea, milk and sugar all in it. All that day riding (about 25 miles an hour average I figure, counting in stops), and all the next night. About dawn after the second night we got off at Bhubaneswar. Daylight. We had passed through the state of Andhra Pradesh, and were now in Orissa. A flat plain

Orissa, Konarak.

of minimum fertility. At one time this had been a kingdom and a cultural center of its own: around Bhubaneswar are numerous Hindu temples, some of the most beautiful in India. We took a bicycle rickshaw to the government-operated tourist bungalow, which stood alone in a wide field, and were given a clean room with cement floor and bathroom in back, as usual. Could see the towers of temples about a mile off, over cow pastures, so after eating some bread and bananas and tea took off on foot and spent the day exploring some lovely pink-stone architecture and carving, some cave-temples on the outskirts of town which had once been occupied by Jain monks. The main temple, the Lingaraj, was closed to non-Hindus and I couldn't get in. We were walking along the wall of this giant temple compound and a little boy came up and led me to the police station, where they were holding my light meter (the one Harold gave me) and asking if it was mine. Seems I had left it on a stone by the Jain caves (five miles away) and an Indian boy had picked it up and traced me to the Lingaraj temple, and brought it over. I hadn't even missed it. I gave the boy a reward—most grateful.

Train, miles of dry, almost bare baked hard ground crossed by cow or people paths—lone trees—villages, cone or pyramid thatch roof, truly mud walls—pictures painted on the doorstep every morning, and designs drawn around the doorway, in white and red and blue, mixed in a cowdung and water medium. These temple towers more spiritual and virile than south Indian *gopurams.*

Orissa, Konarak, wheel
of the sun-chariot.

19 January, to Konarak. Early morning India—still dark—mysterious p.a. systems switch on bazaar, hot Hindu music, ragas drone, girl voice pours out. Streets opening— haircuts at 6 A.M., milk coffee thrown between brass cup and bowl—bullock cartwheel climbs up and falls over grinding through cowpies—cows dribble shit—tails arched, as they lurch forward, the yoke caught on the neck before the hump. Bony calves straggle after their mothers, deprived of milk—which is sold (Gandhi quit milk thus)—dim huddled figures squat through the landscape, shitting off curbs and dikes and paths between paddy fields—by trees—and gangly bodies head and shoulder wrapped in once-white cloth are treading proudly nowhere, stand straight along the railroad tracks or tanks or cart roads—pacing from green coconut juice to a sandal-wood paste spot between the eyes—women bend down laying white powder lines, intricate arabesque and floral designs before the doorway, streetdirt pattern—to keep out forest spirits, someone said.

The sun half-round and giant red swims in a purplish dust-haze horizon far down miles of cowpath and dry pasture, barren rock hills weird boulder shapes, no water ever worked those rocks over,—catch light, the first cows in the road—Hi! people yells; nobody moves but treads or ambles. Even the bus with its rubber-bulb cork-screw curl brass honker sounds like a cow—they all move down the dust cloud path. Tea and coffee stall kerosene lamps dim out as the sun hits with instant warmth on the whole flat world.

Orissa, a Jain temple cave.

Konarak: far off from the ledge of the temple tower, I could see sandy beaches and sea. To the south, from the adjoining *math* (monastery) come sounds of worship, like a party gone wild with beating rhythms on pans and gongs—this *math* worships *sunya,* emptiness, the only known Hindu place left that does—a clear hangover from the days when Orissa was all Buddhist, and emptiness was everywhere.

Naked couples making it in the difficult ledges and cornices where they can hardly be seen. Once a river and a seaport here, but the Sun Temple and the Lord of the Universe (at Puri) couldn't keep the river from silting up, changing course, and sand from creeping in from the ocean, over miles of once-cultivated land.

Busride to Konarak from a big tree in front of the Lingaraj temple. Through real hinterland. Mud and wattle, bamboo used as rafters in the thatch. Doorframes set and plastered into the mud walls. The erotic elements at Konarak are strangely subdued, when seen in the context of the structure's mass. In frieze after frieze, girls kneeling sucking a man off, while he embraces a second girl, standing.—Each time one moves in on a new temple one strains to grasp the layout/scheme of it all, while appreciating details of sculpture and decoration. Aesthetic pleasure as a grasp and delight in grasping created form. But something more—the form moves toward something: in the south Indian temple, *gopurams* (towers) are on the outmost wall, and diminish in size in the inner walls as they approach the center. The temple is always receding from you. In north India the biggest tower is at the center, over the holiest spot.

Konarak closeup.

Culture as a matter of "style" that pervades. Why does a tribe or caste cling to a certain color and design in its clothes, jewelry, pottery?

IX. *Calcutta*

FOR PICTURES AND ARTICLE about Konarak see *Evergreen Review* #9. That night we went back to the railway station and took the train on for Calcutta. All night sitting up, hunched over, Joanne in a parka, me with sleeping-bag cover draped over, getting chilly for the first time. Calcutta by daybreak. Taxicab to the Mahabodhi Society headquarters, a Buddhist society, where they gave us a room. We stayed here five days. Calcutta is an incredibly grim, dirty, poverty-stricken place. But we had lodgings, and needed some time to catch up on things—went to tourist bureau and got information for the next stages of the journey; Nepalese consulate and got visa for Nepal; Calcutta Museum, full of splendid statuary including most of the railings from the great Buddhist center of Barhut; an evening and dinner at the home of Buddhadeva Bose, one of Bengal's leading modern poets and publisher of magazine (in Bengali), *Kavita*. Big pro-and-con discussion on whether modern Indian poets should write in English or their native tongue. Bengali poets are convinced they are the best Indian poets, and have the best Indian language for poetry. They are also still hung up on Tagore, who

Bodh Gaya.
The Thai Temple.

I think is a drag in English, but they said he is infinitely better in Bengali, to which I replied he'd better be. Bose, his wife, his daughter and his son-in-law all jolly people, drinking whisky and talking international intellectual gossip. How lonesome such people must feel (with a certain nostalgia about the British even) unless they can turn again, losing themselves in India's present-day culture and problems. With pleasure left Calcutta on the evening of January 26, in a third-class compartment full of crazy Punjabi muslims going back home, a mountain of luggage.

X. *Bodh Gaya*

RIDING THE "UP DOON EXPRESS"—Joanne slept on newspapers in the aisle, I sat crosslegged over bundles. 6 A.M. in the town of Gaya, Joanne and me off. Still six miles to Bodh Gaya, the place where Sakyamuni Buddha achieved enlightenment. Outside the Gaya station, first sight of Tibetans, camped in the shelter of an old building under a verandah roof. Droopy wine-red coats tied up at the waist, felt and leather boots. They have indeed the famous warm "rancid yak butter" smell, mixed with old leather—not unpleasant! And they are dirty with long greasy hair and heavy jade or turquoise jewelry. The weather noticeably cooler here than it was in the south, Joanne was wearing a shawl she'd bought in Calcutta, and me my sweaters.

Left: The Tower at the Bodh Gaya Temple at the spot where the Buddha became enlightened.

Below: Tibetans at Bodh Gaya.

Bodh Gaya: Rickshaws push around—but we want to take the bus from Gaya to Bodh Gaya—after walking a turn round the square before the railway station, and seeing no bus stop, we have tea (next to a man neatly preparing to make up the day's supply of betel to sell—washing off the mixing board, and bronze utensils shiny and ready)—Joanne takes a double portion of milk tea in her tall white enamel cup, then I go look back of the brick shed where the Tibetans are sacked out—husky ragged-haired kid far taller than me, can't make out if it's a girl or boy—mukluk-like boots, he looks and smiles at me—I walk over a floor of people rising and dressing in hunks of sheepskin, tattered felt, rough chunks of silver and heavy beads—long hair, the men's uncombed forever; the women's worked into braid or coils. Through them, and beyond, still no sign of where to catch a bus. Then one Indian comes up and asks what I want. I say the bus to Bodh Gaya. He leads me back across the square inside the train depot and up to the tourist information bureau—it is open now. I go in and there is a young fellow behind a desk talking to a pair of yellow-robed Bhikkus. I ask where do you catch the bus for Bodh Gaya? He says: The bus stand. And that is about a mile away, pay 4 annas for a cycle-rickshaw. I go back outside and ask the first cycle-shaw boy that comes up how much to the bus stand? 4 annas? He says o.k. But he gets lost as I push over to the tea-stand where I left Joanne and our two rucksacks perched on an upturned bench spotted with crowdroppings from the tree above, a rookery. (Why do crows like trains? The third train station I've

*Far left: Along one
wall of the Bodh
Gaya Tower.*

*Left: Bodh Gaya.
The Tibetan
Temple.*

seen since Ceylon with a rookery nearby.) We pick up our gear and start arguing about fare with another cycle-shaw. A Tibetan Lama suddenly appeared with a huge smile saying "six annas." Then I spied the boy who tagged me as I came out of the station, and he again said 4 annas, so off we go with him, Joanne and me both, and two rucksacks. Finally the bus stand. The bus (with all signs written in the Devanagri script, hence incomprehensible) is empty. We get in. The time is now about 7 A.M. The bus is supposed to leave at 7:30, but at 7:10 the bus pulls out (we are eating funny sweet cakes), and after a bit of wriggling about town we are pulling in at the railway station again! Ten or 15 Burmese Bhikkus load aboard. Back then to the bus stand and 7:30 departure. Passing along the road, and along the Lilajan river. Pony cartloads of Tibetans. At the edge of Bodh Gaya village the bus stops and the driver says "Burmese temple"—the Bhikkus clamber out. A long discussion, Burmese layman interpreting, between the Bhikkus and the driver—at length the driver climbs back aboard. A Bhikku comes back up to his window asking "are you satisfied?"

A short ways to Bodh Gaya village, narrowing and dirty, houses and road turn and up a hill the bus halts under a tree. Mahabodhi temple tower on one side, a tent-camp of Tibetans on the other. Finding the Mahabodhi Society building—two Bhikkus, one old and toothless, speaking a sweetly formal English says "I was a Civil Servant in Ceylon, I became a Bhikku in the evening of my life." The other, his superior, is

Bodh Gaya, Thai temple.

Tibetans camping.

Far left: Making dinner out back in Bodh Gaya.

Left: Tibetan family at Bodh Gaya.

younger, darker, and speaks less English. They give us a whole hall to sleep in, with one side being rooms full of Tibetans (doors opening on the outside) and on the other, the Bhikkus in one room and a Ceylonese brother and sister in the other. The rest of the day we spend here—napping in our sleeping bags spread out on mats on the concrete. Rising late in the afternoon, we went out to buy vegetables, built a small brick fireplace in the backyard, and cooked a ghee-vegetable stew, hot with chilis, fired by awful trash, to eat with fresh heavy round loaves of Tibetan home-baked bread from tent-bakeries in the campground next to the Tibetan temple. Then, in the end of the hall, to read a while and early sleep.

Bodh Gaya is part normal Hindu village, and part archeological site cleaned up by the Indian Government, with the Hinayana and Tibetan pilgrim throngs camped around it. After many years of litigation the Mahabodhi Society has control of the temple itself, which dates back to sixth century, although from the time of the decline of Buddhism on it was under control of a local Hindu monastery. Tibetans are doing circumambulation *(pradakshina)* around it day and night, whirling their prayer wheels. In the shrine room itself you can hear simultaneously the chanting of Lamas and Bhikkus, each in his own style and language. At the foot of the tower, in the back, is the Bodhi tree, descendant of the original. At night the Tibetans from the local Tibetan temple did *puja* (worship) here, with burning ghee lamps. The Thai and Chinese also have temples, each in their own architectural style. It was cool and

Nalanda site. Ruined Stupa.

Near Nalanda.

Gary at the cave where the first
Buddhist Council was held.

even rained once in Bodh Gaya. The last morning before we left I got up early and
went and sat behind the Bodhi tree a while.

XI. *Nalanda & Patna*

27 JANUARY, we caught buses north, about five hours riding, to the tiny town of
Nalanda, site of the ancient Nalanda University—headquarters of Mahayana Buddhist philosophers between the sixth and twelfth centuries—and a New Nalanda
University teaching Buddhist philosophy in several languages to laymen and Bhikkus
and Lamas. Claude Dalenberg had given us a contact here—a Japanese man teaching
and studying. We met him, and he got us into the guestroom of the school immediately, and arranged for us to eat with those students who didn't cook their own food
but ate in a common mess. Vegetarian, of course.

This school has about 60 students, from Ceylon, Cambodia, Thailand, Burma, South
Vietnam, Japan, Tibet and India. Almost all are monks. The graduate students, working
in Pali or Sanskrit, are very sharp, scholarly types—in fact, most Buddhist monks from
those countries these days seem to be scholars. (The Japanese student was Hojun Nagasaki,
studying Buddhist logic, the work of the poet-monk-logician Dharmakirti.) We stayed four
or five days at Nalanda. The first day we went to the ruins of the ancient city of Rajagriha,

Rajagriha.
On Vulture Peak.

about six miles away, in a curious basin formed by a circle of steep hills, which was the capital city of the kingdom of Magadha, a powerful kingdom in the time of the Buddha. Today there is nothing left of it but the ruins of some outer walls and some footings, the rest is scrub jungle, monkeys, rocks. It all looks so arid now that one can hardly believe the old literature which described it as well-watered, and the surrounding countryside covered with groves of trees—especially mango groves. A terrible deforestation went over India, one of the reasons it was a richer country 1,000 years ago than it is now. Part of the problem is goats—around the base of every tree the government plants along the roadside or wherever, an elaborate guard fence must be made, usually of brick or an old oil drum.

In the basin of old Rajagriha we climbed up a hill and saw the cave where the Buddha lived many years after his enlightenment, a place called "Vulture Peak." Also another cave where the first council was held after the Buddha's death; and a Japanese Buddhist temple at the foot of the hills, where a tiny priest with big eyes and soft dark eyebrows, a Nichiren-sect Japanese has been living for years beating on his Lotus Sutra drum.

29 January, the following day, spent at the nearby ruins of Nalanda, and the archeological museum. The museum curator, Mr. Sen, was very nice to us; took us through the excavations and later we had coffee with him and his wife—nice Indian educated people with deep interest in Buddhism, although by tradition Hindu—he had a theory that deforestation caused, among other things, homosexuality. (His

Buddhist scholar Mr. Nagasaki, pony cart bound for the ruins of Rajagriha and Vulture Peak.

example was the case of Baluchistan, which was once a lush mother goddess worshiping agricultural region and is now pastoral desert, with celebrated queer fighting men, maybe like the Pathans, too.)

The Nalanda site is notable for the number of buildings, each on a similar plan, open center courtyard with outer rim of cells for the monks. Apparently were four or five stories high. The brick walls are a good six feet thick. They had no arch, so doorways are linteled or corbeled.

While studying through this, Bhikku Ghosananda, a youthful Cambodian, came across the fields holding his robe over his head, and climbed the high Chaitya to join us, then led us out across some farmland to view a statue of Marichi ("Mother of the Buddhas") a big stone slab half leaning over in a field—exotic Mahayana Goddess, bare-breasted (as they all are), holding a noose, a flower, a sword, and riding a flock of pigs, haloed in fire. Close-grained gray stone; from there we walked through an Untouchable village, to the noise of a squealing pig getting shaved. The village was very neat and clean, although the houses were smaller, and made with poorer materials, than the usual village. The people looked at us with very interested friendly faces.

That evening, by request, I gave a talk on Zen training to the students at the university who were interested—about 25 people came, including the museum curator and his wife. Lots of questions afterwards. Flowers in bloom: cosmos, chrysanthemum,

Right: Jain Temple near Nalanda.

Opposite: Deforested hills in Nepal.

calendula, marigold. Marigold are very commonly made into wreaths, or offered on platters to deities and Buddhas. Another evening, with interpreter, talking to nine young Tibetan refugee lamas, they say "Wherever we go we will never forget our religion." By bus, in the afternoon, to Patna. Joanne had a sudden attack of the runs on the bus, but managed to stave it off til we hit a rest stop, took lots of enterovi-oform, and we got into Patna that evening with no embarrassments. Stayed at the Dak bungalow, ate at a little "meals hotel" across the street (Jai Hind). Bright red sunset behind distant trees.

Patna, the ancient Pataliputra, on the banks of the Ganges. The present city is a combination of Muslim influence and the opium warehouses established here by the British as part of the Nepal-China opium trade. Good museum:—Yakshi half-sphere breasts, hard black stone worked like bronze; horseman mustache, Central Asian Buddha. Many arms. Design dangles over the pelvis; circle of flowers. Hands holding bow, sword, flower, vase, noose, vajra. All acting at once; trampling something underfoot. And a quote from a newspaper article, by Mr. Ram Manohar Lohia, head of the Indian Socialist party: "What I have in mind is a single party with the single-minded aim of the new socialism, that is as revolutionary as it is non-violent, as steeped in world views as in nationalism; and a propeller of all the revolutions now going on in the world."

XII. Nepal

HOW TO GET TO NEPAL overland from Patna: cross the Ganges at Mahendraghat, take train to Muzaffarpur, then train to Sagauli, change and take train to Raxaul, on the border, and another train to Amlesganj, in Nepal; bus from there to Kathmandu. 3 P.M. we left from Mahendraghat in a coal-burning fire-tube-boiler paddlewheel ferry. Not only across but upriver a good ways. Square tin kerosene-can mud-and-rod coal stoves on the after third-class deck, men making patties and deep-fat frying. A crowd of dhoti-dressed mustached sooty unconcerned men.

Onto the train, in a compartment with a dusty little low-caste family, the mother in a ragged gray sari, with a little two-year-old girl with only a shirt on, dusty hair, crying—Joanne gave her a banana and she stopped—all night on the trains, slow and grimy. At 5 A.M. in Raxaul, and the moon rising just ahead of the sun (the great conjunction of planets was approaching). We walked across the border to the Nepali train, where the Indian emigration official didn't want to clear us out of the country, said he didn't have time. A leather-jacketed bearded European type jumped out of the train and said he'd just fixed his passport and why couldn't he fix ours. So the man did. Then the train started up, a really narrow-gauge, no glass in the windows, and full of Tibetans heading back for the hills. We pulled along for two and one-half hours at about seven miles an hour, through *terai* jungle. Then into a strange cross between

Right: Bhaudnath Stupa in Kathmandu. Where yaks, cows, and ponies are led in circumambulation to improve their chances for enlightenment.

Far right: Kathmandu. Buddhist Bodhisattva Tara at Svayambhu Temple.

a truck and a bus, and a twelve hour ride up to 9,000 feet and back down again on the wildest twistiest road I've ever been on. At 3 P.M. that afternoon (3 February) all the visible planets plus the moon and sun went into conjunction and the whole Indian nation was convinced the world would be destroyed. The Brahman priests had been giving sacrifices and rituals for some days previous all over the country. So naturally we looked out the windows as we passed through some snow on the ground to see if the world looked any different.

Nepal has intensively cultivated land; ricefield terraces up steep hills, and farms perched on the edge of abysses. Erosion is a problem here too. We were excited as we crossed over the pass, and could see across range after range of farther blue hills, above that white clouds, and above those, the Great Himalaya, so high in the sky and so far away. The Tibetan men spontaneously broke into a song as the bus started downhill again, the sun about to set, the air quite cold, and the snowpeaks towering far across the valley. The visible peaks at that point, as I found out on later research, were Annapurna, Maccha Pucchara, Himalchuli, Manaslu, Ganesh Himal, Langtang, Gosainthan, Dorje Lopke, Dhurbi Dhyaku, and the Everest group.

Into Kathmandu at night, were told where the cheapest hotel was and walked to it, close by, called the Himalaya Hotel. It was so filthy and rat-infested that the next day we moved to a hotel a cut better. The town was very quiet, and most shops were closed, because everyone was awaiting the end of the world. The planets were in

*Firewood sellers,
Kathmandu.*

conjunction for almost three full days and all that time people were scared. Kathmandu looks rather medieval European, with narrow streets, two-storied brick houses with overhanging balconies, often carved wood decoration on the second-floor windows. The Nepali are distinctive from both Indians and Tibetans (all three types live in Nepal, along with some other sub-hill cultures). They wear little black caps, tight trousers, and rough short-sleeved jackets.

One day we rented a bicycle and rode around the Kathmandu valley looking at a number of old pagodas, Buddhist stupas, and Hindu remnants. The buildings and homes all look run down, as though about 200 years ago was the creative high point. Saw groups of Tibetans who had just come down out of the mountains and even from Tibet directly, walking down the trails into the valley. We must have been the first Westerners some of them had seen. We sure stared at each other—them with their pack frames and huge loads, leading little long-haired sheep. Another day took a jeep with another American (who had once heard me read at a poetry reading in San Francisco) and climbed up to a hill, Nagarkot, from which a good view of Everest is supposed to be had. It was clouded over and raining by the time we got there. A disappointment. But enjoyed walking through the hillside farms and villages. The peasants breaking the clods of their heavy soil with wooden mallets. Kathmandu water is full of mica, and gives everyone the runs. More foreigners here than we had seen any place else. There is an easy, inexpensive plane

Right:
Bhaudnath eyes.

Far right:
Weavers outside
Kathmandu.

flight from Patna. The Swiss Aid Mission makes delicious cheese, we bought two pounds of it.

The market, early morning, in the open on the stone-flagged square: young men bring in enormous loads of firewood on their backs to sell; they are barelegged and barefoot, though the hills around town and right down to our level almost are covered with snow (one morning). I bought curds, and an orange that was so bright and juicy looking, but turned out to be bitter and all seed. Cracked barefeet, calloused thick stubby toes. Dinner one night with a Buddhist man who runs a private school and has been to both the U.S. and Japan. He served us buffalo meat and distilled rice-wine called *ela*; we had a very long and profitable talk with him. Sees there is a movement afoot to reform the Buddhism in Nepal (as it sorely needs) and they even have some Hinayana monks there now.

The last morning in Kathmandu, leaving, I went back to a shop in which I'd seen a *tanka* painting I couldn't forget, bargained some more, and bought it. Then took the bus to the airport, and flew back to Patna—only an hour and a half, by air. Just a small plane. The air full of clouds, so we could not see the Himalaya; but had some spectacular views of perpendicular farms and isolated mountain-top houses. When the plane landed in Patna it was a scramble to take off shirts and sweaters. Suddenly the sun was bright and the air very hot again.

XIII. Banaras & Sarnath

FROM PATNA direct to Banaras, the same afternoon catching a train—and getting switched to another train midway on account of a train wreck down the line somewhere—Banaras RR station about 9 P.M.—stayed the night in the waiting rooms. There are waiting rooms for both sexes, in all three classes; when it came to waiting rooms we usually went into the first- or second-class ones because being Caucasians we would never be questioned—my conscience hurt me a little thus exploiting being white, but one can't afford *that* much conscience—because they had showers to clean up in, and long couches you could sleep on. In the morning Joanne wasn't feeling well, a strange ailment she had gotten once before, one night at Bhubaneswar, so we took railway retiring room upstairs and she laid down to sleep it off (after swallowing the various antibiotic pills I had in my first aid kit, and an extra dose of vitamins). I went out and explored the scene, taking a pedicab to the center, walking out onto the Ten-Horse-Sacrifice Ghat, and looking up and down the Ganges at its most sacred point, lined with bathers on the stone steps. Also looked up the headquarters of the Sarvo-daya (Vinoba Bhave's) movement, at Raj Ghat, and made arrangements for stopping at their ashram later. Banaras is medieval-type city with narrow winding alleys—one famous alley lined with bronze and copper utensil sellers—almost got lost in there (actually did get turned around 180° in the alleys of Kathmandu one evening).

Banaras (most anciently Kashi, then Varanasi, or Banarasi, called Beneres or Banaras by the English) has few temples, and those it does have are of little aesthetic interest. The Moslem rulers suppressed Hinduism in a variety of ways. The interesting thing about the town is the air of piety about it, and the fact that besides being a pilgrim center, it is the center of orthodox Hindu intellectual life. Banaras Sanskrit University and Banaras Hindu University. Banaras Brahmans, and some of the South Indian Brahmans, are supposed to have the purest pronunciation ("totally uncorrupted" in some views) of the Vedas. This is important, because the language of the Vedas is the divine language, and magic resides in every phoneme; for the Vedas to be efficacious, they must be pronounced properly or all is lost.

That evening I went out from the railway retiring room to search for bread, bananas, and curds, and on the way back was attracted by a roped-off shrine decorated with flowers and full of men singing and dancing—in fact, I had seen them doing the very same thing that morning, so was curious. Approaching the wall I was gently seized and transported within the paling, decked with a flower lei, had a red spot of vermilion powder placed on my forehead and told to sing and dance with the rest. They were all high (on bhang, a marijuana-milk-honey and nut drink, I presume) and worshiping the Goddess Sarasvati, whose day it was. When one of the men told me it was Sarasvati we were worshiping I joined in quite happily, because Sarasvati is the Goddess of learning, music, and poetry—in other words, the Muse. She is worshiped in Japan under the

Opposite: Varanasi. Edge of the Ganges.

Right: Varanasi. Along the river.

name of Benten, and is wife to Brahma. Turned out those men were all under a vow to sing and dance before Her for 24 hours unbroken and had the one more night to go. They moved with little shuffling steps, some of them hitting tiny brass cymbals to set a rhythm; on the edge were two drummers; they sang a complex melody. The dance increased in pace gradually, and they would sway back and forth—young men, or thirtyish, with mustaches and modern-style haircuts, but wearing the dhoti, and long loose shirt; faces glistening with sweat, great red streaks on their foreheads and heaps of flower leis around their necks—sometimes two or three of them all looking into each other's eyes while dancing with heads tilted slightly back, swaying in rhythm and smiling—until the pace increased to a really frantic rate and they were way out there. The song would abruptly end when it got too fast to hold any longer, and another song would immediately begin, on a slow pace; different melody—and begin to build up again. I got away eventually and got back to the room. Joanne took one look at me with red forehead and leis and thought I was drunk, high and crazy. It took a while to convince her I had just been doing a little worshiping.

Next day Joanne was feeling just fine (12 February); we took a turn through the old section together and a stroll along the ghats. At the Burning Ghat, just like you hear, in books tourists write, they were burning bodies with huge piles of valuable-looking firewood. Firewood stacked around over several acres, and rough junklike boats loaded with firewood, brought downriver from somewhere, moored nearby.

Nalanda,
archeological dig.

The smoke is heavy and dark—and it smells scary if you get it your way, the "smell of burning flesh" is a real thing—all I could see under the smoke was edges of sari, charred leg, and a foot, with the henna'd red sole, still unburned, sticking out. The relatives are squatting around, tending the fire. When I saw how much wood it takes to burn a body I decided it wasn't such a smart custom, in a country where wood is already scarce.

That afternoon took a pedicab (couldn't find out the bus route or schedule) to the village of Sarnath, six miles away. Sarnath is a Buddhist Holy Site. It was here that Sakyamuni went, after getting Enlightened at Bodh Gaya, to find his old fellow-ascetics and tell them what he had found out. In the Deer Park he delivered his first lecture, the explication of the four noble truths, the eightfold path, and the chain of dependent origination. Today the Archeological Survey controls much of the area and has a small museum there. The Lion capital from the Ashokan Column that is the emblem of the modern Indian Government is in this museum, and the stump of the original column is amidst the footings of a large complex of monasteries nearby. Also a very large and interestingly shaped stupa. The Mahabodhi Society has a modern Buddhist temple near the stupa with murals on the inside painted in the 1930s by a Japanese artist. It also has a huge two-floored pilgrim's resthouse across the street, where we proceeded. I hunted up the Bhikku-in-charge, a Ceylonese man, and we were given a room immediately. On the first floor, all the rooms had been semipermanently

Varanasi, by the Ganges. Firewood for cremations.

taken over by Tibetan Lamas, and the courtyard in back was a campground of almost a hundred Tibetans, men women and children. Cooking on little campfires, sprawled out on sheepskins napping, taking their clothes off and looking for lice—some even bathing at a faucet—with their big packboards and loads set up in piles here and there. And how different from the average Indians—who are often sullen and argumentative—laughing and horseplaying constantly. (Sign at bus stop: "2:30 to 1:30. Just time. No bus will come and start.")

There was an English Lama living nearby I heard, so next day, after paying our respects to the temple and stupa, and the Deer Park which is fenced and has four or five species of deer playing around in it, went to visit him. He had been an M.D. and Oxford Graduate; became a Hinayana Bhikku, and then changed to the dark red Tibetan robes "as his understanding of Buddhism deepened." The turning point had come, he says, when the Dalai Lama paid an official visit to Sarnath a few years previously. As he came into the *Vihara* (temple), the Tibetan Lamas were lined on one side of the hall, the Bhikkus on the other—and the Lamas all bowed as the Dalai passed, but the yellow-robed Bhikkus just stood there. After the Dalai had finished his prostrations before the Budda-image, and was starting back out the hall, our English friend suddenly crossed over from the Bhikku side where he'd been standing and stood with the Lamas, and bowed. Later he got a real Tibetan ordination, and was able to spend a summer in a monastery *(gompa)* in Ladakh, then was chased back to India proper

by the government, which has closed Ladakh to outsiders on account the Chinese are trying to take it over. His name is Lobzang (equals "novice") Jivaka. Never heard his English name. He was sincere enough, but I felt making too much of being a Westerner. Although he still hadn't had much actual Tibetan meditation training or philosophical study, he was already preparing to publish a book about his experiences.

Every third Tibetan will try and sell you a coin, a dagger, some jade earrings, or an old *tanka*.

Walking around the stupa, I had noticed an elderly and dignified Lama also doing circumambulation. After a while he approached me, with serene and sagelike countenance, his wispy white beard blowing in the breeze. My heart beat faster as I thought of secret initiations and hidden gurus—he came up to me, smiled benignly, and slipped a handful of Tibetan coins from his robe, inviting me to buy.

At Sarnath
   a Rongbuk, and a
twisty-horned white-bellied
     antelope, some
    elk and deer
      behind barbed wire.

a Lama tries
to sell Tibetan coin
the Grove where Buddha spoke.

15 February, back to Banaras; watching water buffaloes getting bathed in the Ganges—

Monkeys run along window ledges and walls. Seeing out through a screen of leaves.

The far side of the Ganges a desolate beach of sand shimmering midday.

Eat idly sambar, Masala Dosa, at Ayyar's Cafe, a south Indian place—

Bull eating *puja* flowers spilled out from some shrine on the ground.

A line up of beggars; faces screwed into *samadhi* of misery; they make this their lives, refusing to be human, and that is their real tragedy—fingerless, legless, eyeless (there are something like two million blind in India); blind man about 35 sitting on the pavement, grimacing and weeping to no one in particular, his crotch uncovered, a black penis and balls, a rather handsome face.

Three-legged cows, a bitch-dog with her insides half-out her vagina, running about. Flies on it.

And handsome young *sadhus,* with long curly locks and orange-yellow shawl and skirt, and necklace of seed beads; trident or spear in hand, sandalwood paste and red powder design on the brow; dropping a drop of Ganges water on the tongue—holding the ears folded over, touching the brows, the bridge of the nose, with the water.

Camels carrying loads, swaying and padding forward—madhaired children with their crotch tied in weird rags.

That night stayed at the Sarvodaya Ashram in Banaras. Arrived about 11 A.M.; after lunch in the communal hall of rice, vegetable curry sauce, and curds, with chapatis on the side; I wandered around the buildings. Some of the Sarvodaya ashrams are service ashrams, and the inmates spend their days farming and helping peasants improve conditions, digging irrigation ditches, teaching sanitation, and so forth. This ashram is the headquarters administratively, so the members spend lots of time doing secretarial type work, and handling the publication of magazines, books, and pamphlets.

    Lunch: Take shoes off, go into cement-floored high-ceilinged room. As at Pondicherry, we use *thali* (i.e., trays). These are set out before two parallel strips of woven jute matting, on which everyone sits crosslegged to eat. Before the meal starts, a young man gets up at one end and chants something brief, ending with

Om—shanti—shanti (Om—peace—peace—). Serving man then comes down the line dipping out gobs of spinach onto the trays with a big spoon from a bucket. A second time with another bucket, laying two chapatis on each tray; followed by a server ladling out hot *dal* (a kind of thick soup made out of yellow lentils served with all Indian meals) into the large steel cups. A steel cup full of water is on the left-hand side of the tray. Eat with right hands; Indians won't use the left hand even to help tear up the chapatis. Hell, left hand's as good as the right, I sez to myself, finding it impossible to tear chapatis right-handed alone. More chapatis are served as we eat, and a second of the spicy spinach. Then rice comes around. Good to dump the dal into. Last they bring a steel cup of curds, with some homemade molasses in it. All very delicious.

After lunch I wander out, and see on the porch of the cottage next to our building an elderly grizzled-white short bearded man sitting crosslegged doing hand-spinning of thread on the typical Gandhi spinning wheel; a girl of about sixteen with a beautiful sullen face and a scar on her forehead sitting near him. I go up on the porch, and he tells the girl to bring out something to sit on; she gets a zabuton-size red mat and throws it down next to him. I watch: he holds cotton batting in his left hand, turns the spinning wheel with his right, constantly feeding the twirling spindle. He says "This is an Ellora *charkha* (spinning wheel). Gandhi-ji named it after the prison. He used it a lot." I tell him this is the first time I've seen someone

Khajuraho couple.

actually using a *charkha*. He has heard we're from Japan, and asks about it—has heard a lot about Zen. Krishnamurti, who has a school adjoining the ashram, gave a series of lectures this year and spoke a good deal on Zen, and this man went to hear him speak. He says "I have been spinning since I entered public life. After I graduated from college I went and asked Gandhi-ji what I should do. He says, 'Can you spin?' The *Charkha* is Gandhi's gift to us." He asks me, "What about Gandhi." I have a hard time answering, finally I say, "Some Americans have gotten a lot out of nonviolence from Gandhi, the Negro movement in the south etc . . ." He breaks in, "You want to *get* something out of nonviolence; it won't work that way. Like India, when she got Independence, she threw Gandhi away." Later I was told this man was Shankarao Deo, a well-known figure in the Gandhian movement, and for a while head of the Congress party.

XIV. *Khajuraho*

NEXT DAY, February 17, left Banaras on the Kashi Express, 1:15 P.M., bound for the little town of Satna. At Satna detrained 11:30 P.M. No retiring room here, so prepared to sleep in the waiting rooms. I went into the men's waiting room, spread my sleeping-bag cover out on a couch and washed up. Joanne came in and said she

had gone into the women's waiting room and went right on into the washroom and started cleaning up, wearing her slacks. An old woman in there started talking to her in some language but Joanne couldn't understand so didn't pay much attention. Finally the old lady left and came back a few minutes later leading some RR stationmen. One asked Joanne in English, "Are you a woman?" She said, "Last time I looked I was," and the men laughed nervously and told the old lady Joanne was a woman all right, and then scolded her for being such a stupid old country lady, and left laughing.

Railway station life—going to the refreshment stand and getting cupfuls of boiled tea in our tin cups; buying *pera* (a kind of candy made of boiled down milk) or *puri* from venders.

Following morning caught a 6 A.M. bus, bound cross country for the ancient erotic temple, Khajuraho. A fine rolling drive through a flat landscape of occasional twisty deciduous-type trees, boulders, distant New Mexico–type bluffs. This is in the state of Madhya Pradesh, a somewhat backward area, with the aboriginal Bhil and Gond tribes still around, and center of Thuggee activities in the 18th–19th centuries. Indian highways are pretty good. At 11 A.M. were at Khajuraho and marched off with our packs to the circuit house, where we got a room. Circuit houses were originally built to accommodate civil servants and traveling British parties—there is a network of them all over India. Now some of them, as at Khajuraho, have been cleaned up, enlarged,

Opposite, left: Khajuraho. Khandariya Temple.

Opposite, right: Joanne in a niche at Khajuraho.

Left: Detail from the Khajuraho wall.

Below: Khajuraho wall.

and developed into government-run tourist hostels, at very reasonable prices. We spent the afternoon of the 18th and all day the 19th closely studying the ten or so temples, set a mile apart in two groups. These also were built in the 11th–12th centuries, during the high period of Tantric Hinduism, when at the courts of several rulers, as in Madhya Pradesh and Orissa both, the people in control became adepts at sexual yoga and devotees of the Goddess. Hence this great flowering of incredibly elegant soaring stone buildings, carved in intricate detail both inside and out with the forms of beautiful women and men, often embracing and frequently making love in a variety of postures. They are so moving, and true, that under their spell one wonders what's wrong with the world that everyone simply doesn't make love with everyone else, it seems the naturalest and most beautiful thing to do. I took as many photographs as I could, actually cliff-climbing the temple walls. These are Archeological Survey controlled, hence you are allowed to make rubbings and take photographs without hindrance; kept up beautifully with grass- and flower-lined lawns.

Above: Wall of the Khandariya Temple.

Opposite: Khajuraho, Khandariya Temple.

Khajuraho closeup.

The great Shiva temple is a model of Mt. Kailash, where Shiva is supposed to live; hence it is a model of a mountain, hollow, with Shiva inside—and the structure of the towers reproduces a feeling of ridges, gendarmes, sub-peaks; the horizontal molding lines reproduced from the base of the plinth up in a variety of variations are a kind of geological-paleontological system of strata, moving up through animal friezes to the "human" level—fossils of dancers, lovers, fighters with leogriffs—temple wall like a human paleontology laid bare—rising; to the Divine Couples seated in shrines on sub-pinnacles—vegetable, mineral, and animal universes—complete—to the mountain summit, spire of pure geometry, a rock crown like the sun. And also, the lingam—inside, in the center of the hill in a small dark room—the main figure of it all; damp gloom—holding it all, lovers and animals, in history, vertically, to the brilliant light and heat of the outside sun. The north walls of temples mossier, darker, with lichen.

XV. Gwalior–New Delhi

THAT EVENING off by bus again. A three hour ride to the town and train station of Harpalpur. Here they have no electricity; the station is lit with kerosene lamps. Joanne and I get the man to let us into the waiting rooms (a crowd of wild-looking people is

Right: Jain figure,
near Agra.

Far right: Taj Mahal.

sleeping huddled under their shawls on the cement floor) and next morning we catch a slow train to a truckline junction, at Jhansi, then caught the Pathankot Express north toward Delhi, getting off a bit farther up the line at Gwalior.

Gwalior has a fine fortress on top of a cliff-bluff; we climbed up this and examined the architecture—Mogul type—then walked down the backside past some enormous Jain figures cut in a cliff, around through town and back to the station, then hopped another train on up to Agra. Shortrun third-class rides are really crowded. Hunkering down next to a big-bellied gray-haired woman with bare skin under her *choli*, talking to me in English like a motherly old Communist. A Punjabi peasant nearby burst out talking to somebody with a slow rising and falling pronunciation like the peasants in Japanese Kyogen plays. At Agra we slept in the waiting room, and in the morning—as usual checking our rucksacks in the train station—went out to see the Taj Mahal.

Taj Mahal is the sort of thing you gear yourself to be disappointed in—or you don't want to be taken in by it—but it quite surpasses any images one might be holding in the mind. A very fine quality close-grained white marble was used throughout and everything carries a feeling of lightness and coolness, although the structure is very large, and the day was very hot. The Red Fort, also in Agra—in the afternoon—a sprawling complex of buildings along the river, built of red sandstone, in the Indo-Saracenic style (i.e., with arches of the Arabic-Persian type, domes, turrets, etc).

Opposite: Agra. The Taj Mahal.

Right: Bat and sandals scarecrow, near Agra.

Far right: Mathura museum, Kushan era woman with grapes and a winepot.

The Moslems' main contribution to India was this type of architecture, I suppose—and the use of the true arch.

Hopped a train again, on north, another short run to Mathura. Mathura isn't much now, but it was the center of the Kushan Buddhist art around the 1st century A.D., and the capital of a kingdom in northwest India controlled by the Kushan invaders from Central Asia. We visited the museum, small but containing some first-rate statues and carved railings that had been excavated in the locality. In most Buddhist and Hindu art, the women are bare-breasted, but the Kushan women are practically the only ones who have a naked and clearly defined vulva as well, in a nonprovocative style. They wear lots of jewelry, however, and an elaborate girdle around the waist. There is some controversy among Indianists about the nudity of ancient Indian women—one school holds that everybody was naked above the waist and wore scanty loincloths; another school says that only high-caste or court women went that naked; and a school of modern Indian puritans says that it was all an artistic convention, and in real life ancient women wore as much as they wear today. In any case, modern Indian women are very modest, and usually keep even their head covered with the end of the sari. It may be that much of this was a reaction to the rapacity of the Muslim invaders, who carted off pretty girls whenever they saw them. I'm sure Indian society must have been much more open at one time.

Other miscellaneous cultural notes: Indian men squat to urinate. This may be in

Joanne at the
Khajuraho
Circuit House.

part a kind of modesty; I think it may also be because it is easier to open the front of the dhoti and urinate without getting any urine on it, than it would be while standing up. And no doubt you know about the toilet-paper situation in India: there is none. Instead, every toilet is equipped with a faucet (if not you bring a pot full of water with you) and you wash your anus with water, using only the left hand, after defecation. Toilets are squat-type, like Japan. I had to do this a few times and it works good, if you don't mind getting all wet. We preferred to use paper, though. So, running out of what we'd brought with us off the ship by the time we got to Calcutta, I went to a drugstore and asked for toilet paper, knowing a small amount is sold. Two rolls cost an enormous sum . . . about 2 Rs 50 n.p., or almost 50 cents. In the Indian scale of living that is lots of money. I took them back to our room, but didn't feel very good about it. Thinking it over, I realized we could use newspaper, and promptly cut up some old newspapers into neat squares, and slipped them in a plastic bag. Next day we took one roll back to the drugstore and traded it for some soap. We always used medicinal soap in India (which is commonly sold) in hopes of keeping down chances of infection.

Back to Mathura: we had a terrible time there with a pedicab driver who was supposed to take us to the museum, could not find it (or said he couldn't)—finally landed us at the tourist bureau (not far from the museum) and then tried to charge us double what we'd originally agreed on to the museum. These great irritable scenes

Flowers relief in marble, Taj main entrance.

were common, and became more common, as I realized how many ways we were getting cheated. I pale at the thought of how much the average unwary tourist gets cheated in India (it's still cheap, to the tourist's thinking)—and it became a matter of fierce principle not to be done in *too* much. It's part of the process of maturity for the Indian nation—they are very nationalistic and proud of their country, and want to be accepted as equals by all other nations, so of course they have to, as a people, grow out of the cheating-fawning-bullying complex of habits that go with feudalistic, colonial-type social relationships. Something of the same feeling about beggars—I did not give to all the beggars who approached me by any means; never to able-bodied adults, and never to children. They are growing up in a society which is gradually eliminating beggars and the need for beggars; and it is doing them no favor to help set them in a pattern of professional begging when the whole thing will be made illegal and eliminated (supposedly) in about ten more years. Deformed and crippled people are a different thing—God knows there are enough of them. Deformed people and deformed animals, India. Lepers without fingers are a common sight; they stand along train platforms or at bus stops, whining under the windows. In the south, people with elephantiasis are frequent, a great stumpy leg, or two, dripping lymph. Blind people. People with genetic deformities, or sores, or awful ailments of unidentifiable sorts. Gypsy girls of nine or ten carrying babies, hanging around trains and buses. It is a real moral dilemma. The pattern most people follow, in their relationships with

Kushan
Shakyamuni figure.

beggars, goes in three stages (Allen Ginsberg and I, at least, agreed on this): first, one gives money to all beggars. Second, one gets discouraged, and also hardened, and turns against them for their rudeness and importunity; quits giving altogether, and becomes a tough old India Hand. Third, one starts giving again, at least selectively—partly out of surrender to the fact that it is easier to get through some scenes smoothly if you piece them off and move on, otherwise they keep bugging you; and partly because some of them *do* subsist entirely by begging, could live no other way, and are close to starvation always.

Afternoon of 22 February caught a train on the last leg of our Delhi journey, arriving there around 7:30 P.M.

XVI. *Old & New Delhi*

OLD DELHI and New Delhi are one contiguous city. The border is marked by the remains of a wall, and occasional gates. When you pass into old Delhi, the streets become jumbled and narrow—this was the capital of the Mogul Emperors, and has the red sandstone Delhi Fort, the vast Jama Masjid Mosque, and an important Sikh Gurdwara (temple). There are famous bazaar sections in Delhi, especially for jewelry and sandals.

New Delhi, which was started by the British, is very roomy and planned, with the roads all radiating from Connaught Circle. The circle has bookstores, restaurants, the American Express, and a Khadi shop and Cottage Industries emporium. (A Khadi shop is a government-run store selling essentially *khaddar*, village-made cloth which is both handspun and handwoven. This is the continuation of Gandhi's hand-spinning program to help provide employment for villagers. They also sell handmade soap, honey, paper, and a few other such items. A Cottage Industries store sells a wider range of products in which the fabrics are handwoven but the thread not necessarily handspun. One becomes very conscious of all the details of fabric in India, they seem to be all hung up on it. Also sell more touristy things like handmade jewelry, decorated sandals, woodcarving and ivory carving, etc. Every Indian town of any size has at least a Khadi shop. They are usually the most interesting places to shop, and the prices are set, and fair.)

So: we got off at New Delhi station and took a taxi to the Birla Dharmashala, which we had heard was a good place to stay. Dharmashala equals pilgrims' hostel. This was an enormous place of pinkish stone, with elaborate white-marble trim, a modern Hindu temple, Buddhist temple, hostel and Hindu-Disneyland garden all combined. All we saw was the big high walls and iron gate, though, when we got there. At first they said we were too late, and they didn't have any room. The gatekeeper was a tall man with a handlebar mustache and a yellow turban. Then they realized we were

Joanne, Allen Ginsberg, Peter Orlovsky, and a little girl at the Jama Masjid Mosque in Delhi.

depending upon them, so they let us in, and took us upstairs in one of the buildings and gave us a bedless room—we rolled out our sleeping-bags and were grateful enough. Next day we got a regular room, on the second floor, and it was quite luxurious, even with a rug on the floor. Turns out they have plenty of rooms, but because we were Caucasian, had felt constrained to give us one of their deluxe second-floor hostel rooms, and since only ordinary hostel rooms were available the night before, had given us nothing but a floor. Mr. Birla is a pious Hindu millionaire, who has built dharmashalas all over India (the Buddhist resthouse in Sarnath was also built by him) and the Delhi "Birla Temple" is his crown. It is very vulgar, but certainly a lively place, with music and chanting going on day and night, and a great commotion of people in the courtyard, many of them bathing or dressing semipublicly.

Our first move was to go to the American Express and see what mail we had. We'd been out of touch all the way from Calcutta. Among other things, there was a note from Allen Ginsberg, saying he was in Delhi and staying at the Jain Dharmashala. So we had finally made connections with Allen. The plan originally had been for him and Peter Orlovsky to meet us in Colombo, and travel together from there on. He had been in Israel around November. As it turned out they had problems with the Indian visa, first, and then with getting a cheap ship from a Red Sea port. They finally had to take a ship to Mombasa, and were hung up in Kenya for about three weeks waiting for another ship coming across the Indian Ocean to Bombay. From

Allen, Peter, and Joanne. The Mosque courtyard.

Bombay they went directly to Delhi, expecting us to be there around the sixteenth of February. So they had been there a week already when we arrived. They weren't in at the Jain resthouse, where we immediately went (on Lady Hardinge Road) so we went about our business, leaving them a note. That night, at 10 P.M. they came up to the Birla, and we had a great reunion.

Next morning we met a couple Americans who were staying in another room down the hall—Tom Leary and Bob Downs, both from San Francisco and both painters. One of them (I forget which) said he'd met Thea in the laundromat in Mill Valley, and had been told to look me up in Japan. Ha ha. Also ran into a couple people from the ship, the *Cambodge,* in the American Express that day. Allen and Peter had been spending lots of time sneaking around Old Delhi and had made connections, through a Jain jeweler, for morphine and opium. Drugs are almost uncontrolled in India—hemp is legal (i.e., marijuana) and the common pastime of villagers—any druggist will sell you morphine ampules if you say you are suffering from kidney stones and need a painkiller. But this was not the important side of their activities; they had just wandered a lot and met a lot of people, and were immediately enchanted with India, as indeed any fairly flexible person would be, since it is a very permissive place in most ways, and everyone has diverse clothes, beards, sandals, weapons, ragged bags and religious beliefs.

While in Delhi, staying at the Birla Dharmashala, we went and visited Kushwant

*Novelist Kushwant Singh
and his daughter.*

Singh, a Sikh novelist and shortstory writer (has had some things published by Grove in the U.S.); and Chattur Lal, a *tabla* (two-drum set used in classical music) player who works for All-India Radio when he's not out on concert tour. Kushwant is a funny, cynical fellow who says all the Hindu mystics and holy men are humbug, and likes to drink imported whisky, which he can apparently afford. He has a beautiful slender daughter of sixteen who wears Punjabi costume; baggy tight-ankled trousers, with an overdress which is cut tight in the waist and bodice, and a gauzy shawl. He asked us if there were any people he could introduce us to. Allen said, "Do you know any nice young poets?" and Peter, "Can ya introduce me to some drug addicts?" We were trying to see India from all sides. Chattur Lal has been to America, once with Ravi Shankar. He is always chewing betel, wobbling his head from side to side, and smiling. About the wobbling: A typical Indian gesture, from Ceylon north—to shake your head, like you meant no, except tipping it side to side also, in a very relaxed manner. It usually means yes (or sometimes nondualistic "neither yes nor no"). So at first we were terribly confused when we would ask someone if that was the bus to X and they'd shake their heads no, and then say hurry up, get on! when it started to pull away. (More about Chattur Lal later.)

Delhi isn't a bad place, lots cleaner and roomier than Calcutta, but lacking in good eating places. Either it's fabulously expensive restaurants with guards at the door, or the usual "Madras Hotel," i.e. South Indian cooking, or "Punjab Hotel," i.e. Punjab

Man in a Punjabi restaurant.

cooking. "Hotel" means restaurant only, nine times out of ten. Now these "hotels" often have quite good food, but they are filthy and crowded, and one doesn't relax in them. Bars there are none of in Delhi.

So, storing excess gear in a locker at the Birla, the four of us left Delhi on 28 February, bound for the Himalayan foothills and the ashram of Swami Shivananda.

XVII. *Rishikesh & Hardwar*

ALL DAY RIDING the bus through rolling level green sugarcane fields, to the town of Hardwar on the Ganges. Transferred to another bus, and after an hour were in Rishikesh, a small town on the flat, just where the flat ends and the Himalayas abruptly begin, and where the Ganges debouches from the hills onto the plain. Hardwar–Rishikesh and on up the Ganges gorge are all exceedingly holy territory. The area crops up even in the Jataka tales, the ancient Buddhist-folklore collection, as the home of mountain-dwelling holy men *(rishis),* magical monkeys and elephants, and wide groves of mango trees.

The elephants are gone, but the monkeys, rishis, and mangoes are still there. Swami Shivananda (equals "Bliss of Shiva") founded the Yoga Vedanta Forest Academy 1936, and has been the head of a large and active missionary Yoga-Hindu organization ever since. They have branches in southern California, and in San Francisco too, I believe. We didn't get to the ashram until about 9:30 P.M., and were led into a big room in the basement of a jumble of half-finished brick buildings on the banks of the Ganges and just within the gorge, so steep; it was full of people sitting crosslegged on the floor—but not in proper meditation posture—while a giant man in a camel-hair coat lay stretched out on a kind of couch with his head propped up, saying OM . . . OM . . . a totally shaved head and face . . . we were at the end of the evening *darshan.* They served everyone hot milk and fried chickpeas, and the Swami asked a few questions about us, like, "Do they have these (chickpeas) in the United States?" (A. Ginsberg said, "yes.") Shivananda was then half-lifted to his feet by two junior holymen, who helped him step by step walk out and to his quarters. He is well over six feet, and in his eighties, and must have been an overwhelmingly vigorous man in his prime, to judge by the energy he exudes even when half-crippled. One of the men led us to a building on a hill above the main complex and gave us a dusty room, and brought a pail of water.

Our building was named Mt. Kailash, after Shiva's abode. (Mt. Kailash is also a real mountain, in Tibet, just over the border from the Almora-Garwhal district, and up til last year by special arrangement Hindu pilgrims were allowed to walk around it.) The following day we sniffed around the ashram, which seemed a very vague place; found a Shivananda Ayurvedic homeopathic medicine store on the premises and bought some Swami Shivananda toothpowder, some Himalaya honey, and had lunch in the dining hall of the usual vegetarian sort, only less. Then we were told we would have to leave the ashram the following day, because a huge crowd of guests would be expected shortly for *Shivaratri,* the night of Shiva, but that we could probably find lodgings across the Ganges at another ashram which was really a hostel, because it had no teacher and no particular program. We got the ashram yoga-teacher, a young South Indian named Shivalingam ("Phallus of Shiva") to give us a private lesson in the afternoon, on the roof of Mt. Kailash. We enjoyed it immensely, rolling our eye-exercises and mouth and tongue and lip exercises. As well as about 20 other postures. I had done occasional hatha-yoga over the last three years, and I'm sure it is of some benefit, just keeping one limber internally and externally. None of the postures he showed us were impossible or dangerous. Allen and Peter walked into Rishikesh, came back bearing sweet rolls, bananas, and oranges.

Evening, the program in Shivananda's room—a series of Swamis got up on a dais and read or recited inspirational-type pieces. Shivananda would cut them off when he got tired, or their time ran out, by saying OM . . . then they all chanted something, and Shivananda gave Allen G. a copy of his book *Raja Yoga* and to each of us (Joanne sitting on the other side of the room with the women, a group including four or five Westerners in sari) a white envelope containing five rupees. We still don't know why. The tone and style of Shivananda's place is very vulgar and most of his followers seemed duds, but his henchmen, and his books, were quite sensible. He is teaching a basic, simplified form of yoga meditation on the basis of Vedanta metaphysics, and nothing could be sounder, except perhaps Buddhism. Zen came into being as a development of the Yogachara sect, which was a sect combining yoga-meditation and Mahayana metaphysical speculative-type philosophical systems largely developed at Nalanda. Also, Shivananda's little giveaway book, *Light Power and Wisdom*, is very funny, where he describes himself: "I am ever happy and joyful and make others also happy and joyful. I am full of educative humour. I radiate joy through humour. I respect all . . . I always speak sweetly . . . I do meditation while walking and while at work also . . ." for about ten pages. He was an M.D. in Malaya for ten years, before becoming a *sannyasi* (world renouncer).

Next morning we moved to Swarg (Heaven) Ashram, across the Ganges from Shivananda's place. Free rowboat service 12 hours a day. Given a room, we went down to the Ganges and took a bath, washing our sins and dirt away. It was very clear, and quite cold. All our clothes spread out on the rocks, we all napped in the sun. Here and there along the river bank, yellow and orange robed monks came down to the river for bathing or water. The woods were full of little hermit huts, and walking later upriver came on classical sight of matted-hair ash-smeared Shiva-ascetics sitting under trees, quite motionless. All this was making a big impression on Allen Ginsberg and Peter, so that Allen began discussing the virtues of a *brahmacarya* (celibacy) vow; and Peter was considering a switchover from western calisthenics (he used to be a bodybuilder) to hatha-yoga. He would scarcely believe me when I told him I could sit just as still as those fellers under the tree, which brought home to me how alien the notion of meditation is to most Westerners. I had sort of come to take it for granted.

Nice vegetarian restaurant near the Swarg Ashram, where we ate chapatis smeared with pure ghee, and had curds for dessert. A three-thousand foot hill rises directly in back of this place—white hermit buildings and a few other ashrams at the base, some cowpasture, and a big mango grove—we went hunting up there on March 3 for yogis, and found a beautiful curly-haired nineteen-year-old looking man in orange robe who spoke English. He sat in a big swing hanging from a flowering tree on the edge of the hill, with a bank of fresh banana leaves below him. His name was Prem Varni. Allen asked him how old he was, and was told: "earthly time is of no importance . . ." Then Mr. Varni closed his eyes and made impromptu the following poem, which I wrote down sneakily.

> In our eternal journey
> In the path of infinity
> Will shine the mercy of God
> Giver of Freedom and Forgiveness

I can see my . . . heart
But he's only my real lover . . .

At which point Allen interjected "And I will worship him by eating bananas!" Varni,
confused, invited us to "astral lunch."

Crossing the Ganges by rowboat in the evening . . . a drunk hillman, an Englishwoman in sari with an Indian man; two comrades help the Nepali-looking hillman
into the boat; night, and monkeys (or some creature) howl on the hillside.

4 March 1962, a special day. Opening of the Kumbh Mela, a fair and religious
celebration lasting over two months that is held in the town of Hardwar every twelve
years. Joanne wasn't feeling so well, so she stayed to rest at the Swarg Ashram while
Allen, Peter, and I caught row-boats and buses to Hardwar. Showers in the boat ride—
bus to Hardwar—through forests and open acres of recently logged ground, nomad
camps with ponies under the trees. We have to pass through a cholera checkpoint,
everyone without cholera-shot slip has to get a shot right there. In the past it seems
cholera fanned out over India in the wake of pilgrims from the Kumbh Mela.

All wheeled traffic was stopped in the town. On the opening day of the Kumbh
Mela, a parade of Sadhus marches through town and down to the bathing-ghat,
and only after they have entered the water, can other varieties of human beings go
in. This parade was coming—first a caparisoned elephant, led by a stout muscular

stark-naked man swinging a sword and dancing-hopping, his body blue with ashes. After the elephant came about 500 more of these naked men, some bearing tridents or swords, all with long hair and beards. Some were in their sixties or seventies, some looked sixteen or seventeen. They are called *naga sadhus* and they live year round without clothes, hanging out in the lower Himalaya. They looked fierce and arrogant, padding along in the soft rain, chanting something together in a low voice, all stopping and starting again sometimes, sardonic sidewise glances. Some blew conch horns. After the men, a long line of women, wearing orange robes, with shaved heads. Some sad old grandmothers, supporting each other and singing a little song as they limped along. Dust whirls and wind-blasts, blowing off tent-awnings; Peter taking a nap on a stone bench under a bridge—at 2 P.M. the Sadhus finally got down to the Ganges and bathed. Soon as they got out they put new ashes on.

Bus back to Rishikesh, where we wandered around some and did shopping, i.e., sugar, salt, bananas, melon, oranges, pineapple; and hearing the afternoon meal-bell of a local ashram which distributes food to the hermits and sadhus, followed the line of yellow-clad or loincloth-clad (the truly naked ones usually hide out deeper in the hills) men that appeared from various quarters and along the riverbanks and groves, through alleys and lanes to a ramshackle (if brick can be so) old structure and into its courtyard, where some men served rice out of one great bath-size pot, and curry out of another, to the Sadhus who each carried his own food bucket (in

Indian called tiffin carrier). Finally back at Shivananda jetty and crossing the river the rains broke on us. We got a quart of yogurt and went on to our rooms, where Joanne lay reading Kipling's *Kim,* and made a monster fruit-and-yogurt salad, which pleased secret hungers in us all—all we could eat—while thunder and lightning played on the hills and rain burst down. It was truly Shiva's night. Banging faroff doors in the dark.

This is what you should always chant:

hari ram   hari rama
rama rama   hari   hari
hari krishna   hari krishna
krishna   krishna   hari   hari.

it is all repetition of the names of Vishnu. Shivananda says you should repeat it during the day whenever you get a chance, and I saw an old lady who did it all one day sitting on a bench.

On March 6th we climbed the hill back of Swarg Ashram, losing the trail several times on the way, and scaring out a band of wild monkeys. So many trees I couldn't recognize. Near the top we came on several terraced little barley farms. People who live up here are of a different culture entirely from the plains-dwelling Hindus. Not

Saddhu,
in Rishikesh.

entirely; but they have distinctive features, and one of them is no *dhoti*, but a kind of trouser for men, similar to those of Nepal. At the top, eating lunch, could see far off the white summits of the Gangotri-Kedarnath peaks, and possibly Trisul.

March 7th went to visit a Sadhu cave community, up the hill back of us. About five natural caves, each inhabited. One cave, at the back, was beautifully fixed up, with walls built out and rustic touches like a Japanese teahouse. The man in it was a very pleasant old fellow who spoke fine English and had his place neat and pretty; a former college professor. A creek came by right in front, with a specially built in section for bathing in the creekbed. That afternoon left Swarg Ashram, made it through the cholera checkpoint back to Hardwar—walked around town again, and took the 9 P.M. train heading east and south for Bareilly. We were on our way to the Almora district, Almora Himalayas, mainly to visit a German named Lama Anagarika Govinda.

XVIII. Almora

8 MARCH—Barely 4 A.M.—sleep a while in waiting room; at 5 a group on the platform waiting to receive a newly married couple from Delhi, with tents and breakfast settings all laid out; and a red-coated bagpipe band, walking up and down, practicing. A slow train through the terai, gravelly riverbeds; finally the hills begin to rise beyond.

At Kathgodam changed to bus, and a six hour ride up valley and along ridges, through hill villages and hill stations—past an army truck that had just fallen off the road, and the two men in the cab just climbed back to the road with only bloody faces and one a broken arm. (Peter Orlovsky, who used to be an ambulance attendant, took a bit of care of him)—to Almora town, at 6,000 feet on a saddle-shaped ridge, 6:30 P.M. and straight to the Dak bungalow, where we got two rooms.

Almora is, as it turns out, an old town—not a hilltown developed as a summer retreat for the British. The streets are narrow and stone-cobbled, the house roofs are natural slate laid neatly on like shingles, and the wooden house-fronts occasionally well carved. The whole area was under the control of Nepal a few hundred years ago, and the British won a battle against the Gurkhas here in the days before Gurkhas became employees of the British. The feeling is temperate; all around us are plum and peach trees in full bloom. A contact of Allen's, Mrs. Gertrude Sen, invited us for tea—and turned out to be the former Gertrude Emerson, an old friend of Ruth Sasaki's in the twenties. Mrs. Sen has been married for many years to an Indian agricultural expert who apparently also shares her interest in Indian philosophy. He showed us his wheat plots, in which each plant was numbered, where he was working on developing a strain that would produce well at 10,000 feet, for planting in Ladakh. It was very chilly at night, so we got some firewood and rum and lit up our fireplace and felt good.

Himalayan view,
bus ride to Almora.

10 March, breakfast in the back of the Dak bungalow, sun pouring in, birds singing, blossoming tea. A great view down the valley, and a long stretch of white-peaked Great Himalaya. Afternoon we walked up to Kasar Devi, the hill two miles to the west, to the house of Lama Govinda. Pines and deodar; over the crest of the hill an unobstructed view toward the Nanda Devi group, but it is clouded over that way. So after a path through the woods, leaving Allen, Joanne, and Peter to sport a while near a little whitewashed Hindu shrine on the hilltop, I hunted out Lama Govinda's place. He is the author of a book called *The Foundations of Tibetan Mysticism* and another on early Buddhist psychology; German by birth, but for some years an Indian citizen. A follower of the Kagyüpa sect, he is married (such Lamas can marry) to a Parsi woman who paints under the name of Li Gotami. I wanted to talk to him because I'd heard he was experienced in Tibetan meditation and intelligent. Turned out he was delightful, as well—wearing a brown Chinese-style robe, with a little beard, and sitting at a folding Tibetan desk, while his wife was playing "Suwannee River" on a piano as I came walking up. A very lucid man. He said he was half-Bolivian. Peter and Allen and Joanne came in an hour later, and after talking about the nature of initiations in Tibet (*wang* or "power" conferred by a Guru on a disciple), Allen talked at length with him about the psychology of hallucinogenic drugs—mushroom, peyote, etc., and although he had no experience of them, had some very interesting views on the reason for their variably demonic/angelic content.

Walked back to Almora and arrived in the dark. Next morning found the Almora cottage industry shop open; it said it was selling "Tibetan blankets, shawls, rugs, woollen cloth, carpets, musks, furs, honey, wood, furniture, resin, cane, mats, apples." I bought a large Tibetan blanket called a *tulma*—hairy like a bearskin, dark brown, and mailed it on to Japan; and Joanne chose a small rug with a flower design, almost half an inch thick.

12 March, we took a truck-bus from Almora to Kausani, which is just about as close to the Himalaya as we could go, on account of the "inner line" the government maintains at a point about fifty miles from the Tibetan border, beyond which tourists are not allowed to pass without complicated permits. The landscape is steep and hilly, with ridge-tops averaging 6 or 7,000 feet, cultivated in the valleys and lower hillsides. Forest is sparse, and usually just around the mountaintops. This area was heavily forested, Mr. Sen told me, up to about 300 years ago, at which time the need for lumber by the Moguls began to be felt this far into the hills, and a steady process of logging began. Kausani, a small settlement on a ridge and a little higher than Almora. We stayed in a Public Works Department bungalow which faced out across a wide valley below, and had several rhododendron trees (a good thirty feet high) in bloom hard by, and a forest of pines and deodars up the hillside. It was afternoon when we got there, and looking across the valley we could see a high, dark, snow-crested ridge with jumbled spurs coming down, above a number of

Opposite, left: Girl in an Almora window.

Opposite, right: Almora. Kasardevi, little Temple to a Goddess.

Right: Almora. Looking across Anagarika Govinda's house toward Nanda Devi.

lesser ridges. It must have been fifty miles crowflight away. Behind that was cloud. Just toward sunset, the cloud suddenly lifted, and Jai Ram! there was a solid wall of white reaching straight up as high as the clouds had stood, the dark ridge had just been a foothill! And it reached along the whole center of the horizon, picked up again, and stretched both east and west as far as we could see. What was in front of us was Trisul–Nanda Devi–Nanda Kot, all around 21–25,000 feet, presenting the appearance of a solid clifflike wall. In fact the lowest pass along that whole section is something like 18,000 feet. The easternmost peaks are Api and Nampa, in Nepal, and the westernmost Kedarnath-Gangotri, nearing the Punjab. I was stunned by the size of it.

Next morning Allen, Peter, and I got up before dawn, and sat on the porch of the bungalow wrapped in shawls and Tibetan blankets, watching every detail of the sunrise on the Himalayas for forty-five minutes, from the first blue glow to the final full blast of reddish light. It was too much. We spent a whole day walking among the wooded ridges and looking out over the blossoming rhododendron and apricot at those mountains.

14 March we took the beatup little bus again (so low-ceilinged you can scarcely sit up straight) and rode one full day, on the first leg of our return to Delhi, to the mountain town of Naini Tal. Peter astounded the hillpeople riders by singing for several hours—hillbilly and rock and roll, in an authentically nasal voice. At Naini

Api-nampu from Almora.

Tal we took a cheap Indian hotel room for the night, looked around the lake, and took another bus, early the next morning, bound for Delhi. The bus wheeled out and down the hillside, and went through thirty miles of twisty switchback descent to the plains, then we were off, first through the terai scrub jungle, and then across the Gangetic plain, straight toward Delhi. Another full day's ride, we didn't get there until 9 P.M., and slept on the floor of the office of the Jain rest-house because they had no available rooms.

XIX. Delhi Again

ALONG ONE STREET near Connaught Circle in New Delhi are a number of stalls run by Sikhs, Tibetans, and Sikkimese, set up on the ground, selling small statues, jewelry, brass articles, and *tanka* paintings. We spent almost two days in these stalls picking over their bronze statues—small household votive figures—and picked out a few of the best. That's where I found Harold's Shiva, and Jack's Annapurna, and a Tara for Philip Whalen, and another Tara for myself. (Tara is the consort of the Buddha, in Tantric Buddhism—the idea of transcendental wisdom represented as a woman.) These statues aren't very old, because they are still being made as part of a living religious tradition. We went to the National Museum in New Delhi, which is very modern and hiply laid out, on account a lady named Grace Morley, who used to run the De Young museum in San Francisco was specially imported to set it up. I'd say she did a good job; although in point of quantity the Calcutta and Madras museums probably surpass it. Also went through the Red Fort Museum in old Delhi, which has harem rooms and court-audience rooms, and a museum. Another visit was to the Young Lamas Home School on the outskirts of New Delhi, a school set up for refugee Lama-boys who are of key importance in the Lamaist system because of their positions (they are all supposedly incarnations of one bodhisattva or another) and need to be educated properly in Tibetan things as well as western, if the Tibetan religion is not to die out in the next generation. The school was started by an Englishwoman, Freda Bedi, and her Indian husband, and is backed by Indian and Western sympathizers with the Tibetan people. It is not a matter of being anti-Communist for these people, as most of them are at least socialists and their activities helping Tibetan refugees are primarily matters of just helping people (the Tibetans are extremely likeable, and handsome) and hoping to preserve the traditional Tibetan religion, which represents with little alteration the several schools of Mahayana philosophy that were current in India in the 11th–12th centuries, and were eliminated largely by the Turkish invaders. No one seriously thinks the Tibetans will ever get independence again, at least not within our time, and indeed their society was ripe for a number of reforms. If the religion can be kept alive, and purified to some extent, it may ultimately be able to resettle in its homeland, and in the meantime may have some influence on the West as well. We walked in on some little kid-monks having debating practice. They clap their hands each time they make a final point, and then wait for their opponent to answer it.

Evening of 20 March went to hear a classical music concert, two Pakistani brothers singing—Nazakat Ali and Salamat Ali—with Chattur Lal on the tabla. This was the second time I'd heard Chattur Lal play, the first time was when we were in Delhi previously, and had attended a special concert given by Chattur Lal and a woman sarod player (sarod a stringed instrument with many strings played with a plectrum and held like a guitar) in honor of a thirty-year-old "much loved young mystic" Shri Krishnaji, who was giving his last words and then retiring into a vow of lifelong silence. Shri Krishnaji, who was of the longhaired long-bearded variety, spoke for almost an hour on "Silence," and then the musicians serenaded him (he actually entered the vow at 5 A.M. the following morning). The point was the music, however. Complex rhythms and a fantastic structure, building up from the simply stated theme ("raga") at the beginning, and developing to a powerful climax, taking a good hour of solid playing, the sarod-player and the tabla player constantly watching and checking each other, playing together and sometimes tricking each other, because after the statement raga, most of the whole performance is improvisation.

The vocal music works in much the same way. The lead brother started out inconse-

Jaipur. Jai Singh's observatory.

quentially, on a low drone note, and very quietly stated a theme—no particular words to it, just voice. And the tabla player joins in only after about 45 minutes of the two singers playing around. As they sing they use their hands, gesturing in the air, making a picture of the sound. The performance went on til after midnight, the audience and performers getting more and more excited, sometimes everybody shouting *wah wah* when they felt something was extra skillful ("wonderful, wonderful").

XX. *Jaipur*

21 MARCH we took the train out of Delhi again, leaving excess luggage at the railway station, on our way to Jaipur in Rajasthan, about 200 miles west of Delhi. The day was *holi:* a kind of spring saturnalia, and the train man told us to lock the doors and windows of our bogy (it just happened that we had the whole bogy to ourselves). Soon we saw why. Crowds of people, mostly men and boys, were running through the streets throwing colored paper all over each other. The men are supposedly high on bhang on this day, but everyone seemed too violent for mere bhang. Kids kept throwing buckets of water at the train, and since we didn't really keep the windows closed, Allen and I got colored. Later down the line people were throwing rocks and clods at the train so we closed the wooden shutters to save the windows. *Holi* is a

At rest in Jai Singh's observatory, Jaipur.

real wild scene, and not entirely safe. For days afterwards we read in the newspapers about people who had been killed in fights and riots on *holi*.

Jaipur is set in an arid valley, one of the main cities of the arid state of Rajasthan, which fades into sheer desert as it goes westward, a big desert which extends across Pakistan and into Iran. It was a center of Rajput power, and the Rajputs were a spectacular and distinctive warrior-type of Hindu that gave the region a stamp of its own. The city is all painted pink, and there are lots of dromedary camels in the streets. The women wear loose, full skirts in bright colors, with blouse tops, instead of saris, and lots of jewelry. Indian women everywhere have nose rings, one to four earrings, armlets, wristlet bangles, anklets, and toe-rings. In Jaipur had a large and comfortable bungalow so we stayed four days—on one of them going to an old abandoned hilltop fort six miles from town, and exploring its rooms and towers. Old fort called Amber. Dusty heavy brick and plaster, with marble and sandstone trim; a room of mirrors.

haiku

> baby monkey taking first steps
> top of the wall
> back of the tourist bungalow.

Jai Singh's observatory.

    the tonga-wallah   (ponycart driver)
pinches the scab on his
        pony's haunch
instead of the whip

    a sikh boy
    like a wild little girl
      combs his long hair
monkeys wrestle
       in the thorny tree
on top of vulture peak
      nobody all morning
selling flowers.

      scrub jungle and monkeys,
      rajagriha
    barefeet on cold marble
      naked Jain genitals   (Sarnath)
      in the shadow.

Right: Jai Singh's observatory.

Opposite page, left: Jaipur. Tinworkers' camp.

Opposite page, right: The street, Amber.

letting tourists off his back
the painted elephant craps   (Amber)

    lady in a nice sari
       walks quickly, not looking too much
at Khajuraho

on the train
       Sikhs and Punjabis
       tired of looking at Joanne
         put their heads
       between their knees
         and sleep.

—And then what did we discover but that a two-night cultural program was about to be put on in a tent, the first night a celebrated dancer in the southern style, Padma Bhushan Smt. T. Balasaraswathi, and the second night a program of Ali Akbar Khan, the world's best sarod player, and Chattur Lal, the world's best tabla player.

Balasaraswathi is the grand woman of Bharat Natyam style dancing, maybe fifty years old now, and a little heavy, but a grand, graceful dancer and a real woman

(as they say—). She did a dance as the mother of Krishna; the story being that when Krishna was a little boy (he was the incarnation of the God of the Universe, Vishnu) his mother once saw him eating dirt, and went to get it out of his mouth; when he opened his mouth she saw the whole universe in it; and stepped back in amazement. When she did this dance, and the part where she looked in the baby's mouth and saw EVERYthing, it was too much, a real moment of holy awe, the shock of recognition, came across. And all the time she was dancing she is singing in a low voice to herself, along with the music, "Krishna, Krishna, Krishna, Krishna, Krishna, Krishna . . ."

A great wind came up and a rain, and almost blew down the tent. So nearly everyone went home. The few of us who stayed got right up on the stage and watched her do her final dance.

Rajasthan stony hills. Thorny scrub jungle—leaves so sparse on the trees you can see right through the woods. Women with tight red or yellow trousers under their skirts. Naked girl by a pump. Next night, Ali Akbar a bald, solemn-faced intense man, with eyes closed in a trance, while his hands speed up and down the instrument; Chattur Lal angelic and demonic by turns making faces, sweat rolling down and his longish hair flying about—playing games with other, tricking the rhythm, following sometimes, then switching—and after several hours of warm-up they got sublime.

Left: Allen at Tinworkers' camp near Jaipur.

Right: Amber. Jagat Shiroman Temple Gate.

That night took a late train, after the concert (actually having to leave a few minutes before it was over), back to Delhi. Got into Delhi in the morning, put almost all our gear into the baggage room, and went about on chores. At the Annapurna restaurant we met Hope Savage, Gregory Corso's first girl friend and longtime patron, an old acquaintance of Allen's as well. She was wearing a shawl and high-topped lug-soled "hunter shoes." Seems she had been in Aden, Ethiopia, Iran, and then back to India (from another time)—spent January in the Kulu Valley (where it snows); then moved down to Odaipur in February, now in Delhi, wondering where to go next in India. She has been moving about like this for three or four years, always alone. Pretty, delicate-looking with milk-white skin and light blonde hair and blue eyes, she has traveled thru dreadful parts of North Africa and Arabia and Iran without serious harm. She is really a little mad, talking almost hysterically fast, putting on to the Indian people that she is an Iranian, and always suspecting that other people think she is a spy. I met her one night at the Mill Valley cabin in 1958. She was passing through America with a French boy who is long since gone. Her father is a big man in some small southern town. She came to the station that same evening to see us off on another expedition, this time due northwest, to Pathankot and the Manali valley, to see the Dalai Lama.

Left: Peter and children.

Right: Jaipur. Girls at the well.

XXI. Dharamshala

AFTER AN ALL NIGHT RIDE, we arrived at Pathankot, in northwest Punjab, at 5 in the morning March 28. This is the jumping off point for the two-day bus trip to Kashmir. It is not far from the Pakistan border. We turned east, however, toward the mountains. There is a valley system about a hundred and fifty miles deep into the Punjab Himalaya. The first section is the Manali and the second the Kulu valley. They are very beautiful. We wanted to go to the Kulu and walk over a 14,000 foot pass to visit the Tibetan-culture, barren and mountainous Lahoul valley, but didn't have time. So we went up the hillside in the Manali valley, to the 6,000 foot town of Dharamshala, where the Dalai Lama has his permanent headquarters (courtesy of the Indian government) and a sizeable settlement of Tibetan refugees. Lodged in a tourist bungalow. A long gentle slope below us, of green wheatfields, orchards, running water creeks and cascades everywhere. The richest-feeling, cleanest, and airiest region we'd seen in India. Above Dharamshala white-capped ridges rise to 14,000 feet and there are fine deodar forests around. We had dinner at the Lhasa Hotel—a meal of Tibetan noodles with meat in it. (First meat in months, as we had gone all-out vegetarian for a while.) In the evening we all smoked opium, since Allen and Peter had picked some up in Delhi and gotten a pipe as well. It was a funny kind of opium, mixed with charcoal in a little ball to make it burn better. Usual opium is a sticky

Right: Manali Valley, Ghanara Fair. En-route to the Dalai Lama's Ashram.

Far right: Gaddi woman at the Ghanara Fair.

ball you have to warm in a spoon over a candle or stove and then lay a burning coal next to it in the bowl to make it smoke when you inhale. It tasted o.k., and after a few balls Joanne and I retired. An interesting feeling—all night a sensation of being not awake and not asleep, just sort of floating, with pleasant thoughts but nothing of consequence—quite different from the heavy content of peyote with all its visual kicks and bad-take possibilities. In the morning we were all nauseated, another effect of opium. Next morning tried to reach the Dalai Lama's ashram, two miles farther up the hill, but the phone was out of order. So we make arrangements to stay a night in the Triund Forest bungalow, which is a seven mile hike up the hill at 10,000 feet, and go off at the invitation of a young Sikh to a local fair. Walked about two miles along the hillside, through little tributary valleys full of thundering creeks, and above wheatfields with neat channels and ditches leading the clear running water. It was a beautiful day, with just a few banner clouds above us on the snowpeaks.

It was a fair of the local hillpeople, called Gaddis, who are big sheepherders. The men wore robelike tan wool coats hitched up in the belt so that they only hung down to midthigh. The belt is a coil of woven wool rope, which they can unwind and use if they need it. The men wear small gold earrings and little woven caps. The women have a complicated costume and pounds of jewelry, at least on fair days. It was held on a wide, high, grassy plateau. Handrun ferris wheels, goat carcasses hung in trees being skinned out; a bank of drums and drummers, long-haired sheep standing on

Allen Ginsberg drumming at the Ghanara Fair.

top of boulders. "Shakespearean" Allen said—it was indeed anciently and idyllically pastoral.

A series of amateur wrestling matches: an older-looking man, light of build, with one weak polio-affected leg, matched against a heavier, more muscular, younger man. Gurdip the Sikh said the old man would win, but we couldn't see how. They wore tiny jockstraps, and fought in a dirt pit in the middle of the grass. The old man was underneath all the time, but he couldn't seem to be put on his back. At one point he was on his hands and knees, and the big fellow was on his back. The old man reached up and caught him back of the neck, and threw him clean over his shoulder and laid him out flat, then got up and did a limpy little victory dance while the other man got up rubbing his neck and looking sheepish and bewildered—the old guy joined with a little orchestra band marching around the perimeter of the wrestling ground, dancing and hopping along.

Morning of March 30 we set out climbing with our rucksacks. Passing the Dalai Lama's ashram we made arrangements to meet him the following afternoon, then went on climbing up the trail. A long steady climb. Eat lunch by a snowbank. Behind us finally comes the chowkidar (caretaker) of the bungalow, who doesn't live in it full time. He could speak no English, and was kind of a problem for us. The Triund house is on a ridge that climbs up higher toward the main mountains, and drops off steeply on both sides. Spectacular view. This house is really for the Forest Service,

Ghanara Fair, near Dharamshala.

but non-civil-servants can use it if it's not officially occupied. We have a terrible time getting firewood, water (by melting snow) and kerosene lamps. This chowkidar is the most useless creature, just sort of hanging around watching us, and doing nothing himself. Part of the trouble was that it was well before the usual season when people use the place. In the logbook, we noticed that the Dalai Lama had come, with two or three others, seven times up here, often for three or four days at a time. He is always referred to in English as "His Holiness."

In the evening we built a cozy fire in the fireplace. Next morning I got up quite early and left the others sleeping, and pushed up the ridge. It was blowing mist, and pretty soon started to snow lightly. I climbed to timberline and a little beyond, until finally I was on a great snowfield leading up toward the actual peak of the mountain, Dhaulagiri. Instead of an iceaxe I was using a steel-tipped cane I had got at the village below. The wind became extremely strong and I was getting covered with snow on one side, and there was no view whatsoever. So I turned reluctantly back, from my highest elevation in the Himalayas, about 12,500 feet. That wouldn't even get you to the base of Everest. On the way down, in a little nook at the base of two cliffs, I saw a stone platform with splashes of faded orange color on it, and some rusty steel tridents stuck in the boulders beside it. The meditation-platform and living quarters of a Shiva-ascetic, at some time. Back at the Forest House the smoke was coming out the chimney and there was a hot breakfast. Around noon we started down.

XXII. Dalai Lama

THE DALAI LAMA'S ASHRAM has fences around it, and a few armed Indian army guards. Between the tops of the deodars are strung long ribbons of prayer flags. After getting cleared through the guardhouse (and washing up at a pump, right in front of the guards) we were led to a group of low wooden buildings and given a waiting room to wait in. I guess the Indians are afraid the Chinese might come and kidnap the Dalai if they're not careful. A few minutes later the Dalai Lama's interpreter came in, a neatly western-dressed man in his thirties with a Tibetan cast, who spoke perfect English. His name is Sonam Topgay. He immediately started to ask me about Zen Buddhism. It seems he had found a book on Zen (if I understood him right) in a public toilet in Calcutta, and was immediately struck by its resemblance to the school of Tibetan Buddhism he followed. After that we didn't talk about Zen much, but he told me about the Zok-chen branch of Rnin ma-pa (Red Hat) which is a Tantric meditation school. He said it was by far the highest and greatest of all schools of Buddhism, including the Yellow Hat (which happens to be the sect which his employer, the Dalai Lama, is head of). (Don't tell the Dalai Lama I said this.) He is originally from Sikkim, went to college in Delhi majoring in psychology. Got fits of depression and figured out a method of "introspection" to see what was the mind that felt depressed. Then he went to Lhasa and met a saintly old woman age 122 who told him to go see Dudjon Rimpoche of the Rnin ma-pa, which he did, becoming that man's disciple. He also married a girl in Lhasa. He said that one of the good things about his school of Buddhism was that you could marry and you and your wife could meditate together while making love. Then they came out, when the Chinese moved in, with their baby girl. (A book by Evans-Wentz called *The Tibetan Book of Liberation*, I believe, is of this sect. *Book of the Dead*, also.) They also say, perfect total enlightenment can come: 1) at the moment of dying, 2) by eating proper sacramental food, 3) through dance and drama, and 4) at the moment of orgasm.

Then he told us the Dalai Lama was busy talking to the Maharajah of Sikkim, who had just dropped in, and that's why it had been such a long wait. So we went into the Dalai Lama's chamber. It has colorful *tankas* hanging all around and some big couches in a semicircle. We shake hands with him except that I do a proper Buddhist deep bow. The Dalai Lama is big and rather handsome. He looks like he needs more exercise. Although he understands a lot of English, always keeps an interpreter by when talking to guests. Allen and Peter asked him at some length about drugs and drug experiences, and their relationship to the spiritual states of meditation. The Dalai Lama gave the same answer everyone else did: drug states are real psychic states, but they aren't ultimately useful to you because you didn't get them on your own will and effort. For a few glimpses into the unconscious mind and other realms, they may be of use in loosening you up. After that, you can too easily come to rely on them, rather

Game in a leveled field, near Dharamshala, middle Himalaya.

than undertaking such a discipline as will actually alter the structure of the personality in line with these insights. It isn't much help to just glimpse them with no ultimate basic alteration in the ego that is the source of lots of the psychic-spiritual ignorance that troubles one. But he said he'd be interested in trying psilocybin, the mushroom derivative, just to see what Westerners are so excited about. Allen promised to try and put Harvard onto it, and have this professor Dr. Tim Leary send him some.

Then the Dalai Lama and I talked about Zen sect meditation, him asking "how do you sit? how do you put your hands? how do you put your tongue? where do you look?"—as I told or showed him. Then he said, yes, that's just how we do it. Joanne asked him if there couldn't be another posture of meditation for Westerners, rather than crosslegged. He said, "It's not a matter of national custom," which I think is about as good an answer as you could get.

The Dalai doesn't spend all his time in his ashram; in fact he had just returned from a tour of south India, Mysore, where a few Tibetan refugee resettlements are. And last thing I've heard (since I got back to Japan) is that he's going to set out and do some real Buddhist preaching over India, and maybe Europe and America eventually, spinning the wheel of the Dharma. He is at the least a very keen-minded well-read man, and probably lots more than that. Also, he himself is still in training—there are the "Senior Gurus of the Dalai Lama," the most learned of Tibetans, who keep him on a hard study schedule and are constantly testing and debating with him.

Walked back down the hill, two miles in the dark, illuminated by occasional lightning-flash, to our bungalow. To sleep late, some Englishman shouting under our windows.

On April 1, two in the afternoon, we took the bus back out of Dharamshala, our last look at the mountains; hardly had the bus got started and I said "my God I've forgot the cameras!" Joanne turned white and Allen and Peter looked serious. So I said April Fools. Little Tibetan kids running down the street in the black-and-red boots, little robes flying, long braided hair. By evening we were in Pathankot, and took a railway retiring room. I went out and bought some eggs, some bananas, and some orange gin (the Punjab isn't dry). It was hotter than it had been up at Dharamshala. We got one of the sweepers to promise to wake us at 4:30 A.M., because we were going to catch the Pathankot Express, which leaves at 5, the next morning.

XXIII. Sanchi

THE PATHANKOT EXPRESS is one of the great Indian trains. It is broad-gauge (a little over a meter) and runs between Pathankot and Bombay through Delhi, a good distance. It takes two days and two nights traveling. We got settled into a reserved third-class sleeping coach, the only people on it, and were off for a good long ride.

Passed through the rich Punjab farm country, homeland of the Sikhs. 8 P.M. we're in Delhi. During the layover of the train there (we had it planned this way) Allen and I went to the baggage room and got the extra things we'd checked there, stowed them in our coach, and off we rolled. All night sleeping across from us a crewcut white-haired Indian, sixty or so, wearing shorts and barefoot, with some poor-people's type luggage, reading *Doctor Zhivago*. Also a beautiful Sikh *khalsa* stud (*khalsa*—orthodox oldstyle Sikh) about 40, with the totally uncut beard, his turban about a foot high, wearing a flaring dresslike jacket, with "short drawers" under it, earrings, a huge iron bangle, a dagger, and carrying a long sword in a sheath, and a battleaxe. About 12 noon the train stopped at Sanchi—in shimmering heat now, no more of those mountain breezes—and left us in the middle of the wild west. Smallest train station we'd been in yet.

This is the dry plateau, about 1,000 feet high, that lies between the Gangetic plain and the Arabian seacoast, and the plains of the south. Part of the Deccan. The trees are wiry and twisty, in bloom with a scarlet flower. The brown grasses and rocks—it is the beginning of the hot season now, and everything is drying out. No rain until June. Sanchi, one of the oldest Buddhist monuments in India, is on top of a black-rock hill in back of the station. A very large stone stupa, with an elaborate high stone railing around it, and two other smaller stupas nearby, plus the footings and remains of monasteries and various shrines—the stupas relating to the 2nd century B.C. Artistically one of the highpoints in Indian art—especially the elaborately carved gateways at the four quarters of the railing around the main Sanchi stupa, and the bas-reliefs carved on the posts and railings of the smaller stupa no. 2. We looked it over in the afternoon, paying a call on the new Buddhist temple nearby, and visited the Mahabodhi Society center (we were staying in the railway retiring room this time, because we were getting so much luggage we didn't feel like carrying it anywhere).

Next morning, April 4, Joanne went up the hill with her inks and papers that she'd brought from Japan, to spend the day rubbing on stupa 2. Allen and Peter and I took a bus to the nearby town of Vidisha and tonga three miles out in the hills to look at some old Jain and Hindu caves—smell and squeak of bats in old holes—hand-patted clay rooftiles, looking like cowdung cakes. Vishnu as a boar. In Vidisha had tea at a roadside stall which was small and ordinary looking except that it was CLEAN—the pots shined, the tea served with lids on the cups, the man who ran the place immaculate! Zen.

Afternoon back to Sanchi, on the hill hanging around stupa 2, helping Joanne to make rubbings. She made many here, as it was the best place we found in India. Then to the Mahabodhi Society, by invitation, for dinner. The Bhikku-in-charge here is only about twenty-one, and quite handsome. He is not Ceylonese, but an Indian. He ran away from home when he failed college, and somehow ended up in Sanchi broke.

The Bhikku took him in, fed him, and let him have a room for many months—so he ended up by becoming a Bhikku himself, renouncing Hinduism. The big Bhikku was visiting in Ceylon when we came by. The Mahabodhi center there is busy building a library and meditation hall. It looks like it has potentialities, especially since for some reason the feeling of the whole area is so strong even though on the surface it is like any other central Indian vast and barren locale. (I say barren; there are of course villages here and there, but they are mud and tiny, and look like they have just grown up out of the soil, scarcely an intrusion of mankind into the scene; and the cultivated fields are scattered where there is available water, in the midst of large arid-boulder lands.)

We had an unexceptional vegetarian curry. I asked the young Bhikku who the old monk was I'd seen sitting in front for two evenings now, meditating. He said the man was a Tibetan who had been a teacher to the previous Dalai Lama, then had gone to Burma, and later to Ceylon, receiving Hinayana ordinations in addition to his Tibetan ordinations—and for the past few years had been spending the cooler seasons at Sanchi. He said the old man disappeared to the northern (Himalayan) hills when the weather got too hot, and got back in time for the relic-opening (relic was what was in the stupa) ceremony every fall. He said the old man meditated most of the time, sometimes sitting on top of stupa 2 (which is flat on top) or under local trees. He said he was over seventy, and sometimes he would disappear to beg in the villages for a few days, but would never ask directly for money. Wore the sandals and yellow robe of a Hinayanist.

We carried our canteen with us, dipping it in water whenever possible, to keep it cool by evaporation. It really works in a dry climate.

XXIV. *Ajanta & Ellora*

APRIL 5, we got a noon train on down the line, a nine-hour ride to Jalgaon. Stayed the night in the railway retiring room, and took a bus the next morning to Ajanta. Heat on us now, sweating in bed in the night, the fan on, the floor of the retiring room hot. Tea before the bus left in the square before the bus station, loudspeakers blaring music, sweets and tea. Tongas lined up. We got off actually at Fardapur, a good two miles from the Ajanta caves. There is a Dak bungalow here, in the midst of a long brown pasture. The autumnally barren leafless hills a mile away south. Water buffalo calf moos—I love water buffalo, they are vulnerable-looking, whereas the Brahma bulls and cows are arrogant because they know they are beautiful. A German in Madras called water buffaloes "brake inspectors" because they cross highways without paying the least attention to cars or trucks or buses. It's up to you. Unload packs and catch the next bus on to the caves, wash hair in the tap while waiting.

Ellora Caves from the north.

Ajanta caves, cut in the cliffs around a great U-turn in a creek, 24 monastery caves and five temple-caves. The earliest are about 1st century B.C. and the latest 8th century A.D., so you have both Hinayana and Mahayana art. Three or four have walls and ceilings painted—much worn off and discolored and flaked away now, but enough surviving to know that it was a major painting tradition, great skill and sophistication. Reproductions of these paintings give no sense of their size, or the effect they have on one way in the back of a cave. These caves were all excavated, and some of them are sixty or seventy feet deep, with additional cells on the sides; the pillars and entrances beautifully carved. The sheer number of skilled craftsmen it must have taken to accomplish this and other early Indian building projects is staggering. Square doorlight, the heat outside. Deep in the caves cool.

Back at the Dak bungalow at 4:30, we mixed some drinks out of gin and canteen-chilled water. Allen and Joanne had a long talk on Bill Burroughs' writing methods.

April 7, Saturday, took the bus on down the same road, to the town of Aurangabad, after spending half-a-day again at Ajanta. Vultures and bees nests on the cliffs. A deep pool at one end of the box canyon where Peter went swimming. (Painting detail over my head listening to Peter yip up the canyon far away: a man offering a girl wine, over and over, forever.—Like thou still unravished bride of quietness.) At Aurangabad: a wide spread out city on a plain between hills and bluffs—once a

Right: Goddess Ganga River. Ellora, Cave 21.

Far right: Ellora Cave-chamber Buddha and Chaitya.

Mogul subcapital—ranchlike spaces—the municipal Dak bungalow. Breeze blowing through the room in the evening, no fan. "Dry commode," i.e. chamberpot toilet instead of water-flushing. They had a man of low caste whose full-time occupation was to squat at a distance watching the toilet. When he presumed someone had used the dry commode, he was to come to the back door of the toilet, take it out, empty it and put it back clean.

Aurangabad is place to pitch camp for visits to Ellora. Bus in the morning to Ellora. This was a one-day excursion bus, by which we meant to get a general orientation to them. There are about 30 caves, half Buddhist and half Hindu. Cave 16, Kailasa, is not a cave, but a full-size Hindu temple that was built by cutting away all the rock and sculpturing a building. It is estimated that 3,000,000 cubic feet of rock were excavated to build it. Furthermore it was all painted in bright colors once. And the question of all the lovely nude women in the Buddhist art. How did they get away with it. Before it got dark, back in Aurangabad, Allen and Peter and I walked about its dusty downtown—soap, vegetables, curds, bath sleep.

April 9, rented bicycles and rode over the hot ground through a palm tree grove to the hills, and climbed up to the less-known Aurangabad caves. Swam in a stone cave-pool by cave no. 1. Cave no. 7 is full of fine sculpture, a group of six female musicians and a dancer with fat thighs, legs wide and feet turned out, half-globe breasts, and a little instrument in her hand.

Allen at Ellora Cave.

April 10, Allen and Peter and I went for another full day at the Ellora caves. We took them one by one and looked at everything; green-and-purple-sari'd working women at noon rest, one laid out in the shade on her belly indolently nursing a child. The Ellora caves, rather than being built in a canyon carved by a creek, as Ajanta, are cut into the cliffs at the edge of a large plateau, and the caves look out onto an endless shimmering dry plain. Some of the caves have been excavated with three stories, each story with an altar chamber, cells in the sides, elaborately carved pillars (the pillars, too, are part of the living rock) and stairway passages connecting floor to floor. Here also the caves were painted at one time, but only vague flecks of color are still adhering to the rock, on an occasional flower, or part of a human body. Climbing above the caves at one point, and walking along the rim of the cliffs, we found a little stone gully with four or five small caves along its walls that weren't mentioned in any of the guidebooks to Ellora, and several clear pools of water in the gully. So we went swimming. Then back down to the end caves. Bus back to Aurangabad in the evening. Caves are an ideal kind of architecture to last. There's no reason, aside from possible human vandalism, why the Ajanta and Ellora caves shouldn't survive more or less intact, with the sculptured bas-reliefs staying very clear (since there is no wind, water, or sun ever on them to speed erosion) for a hundred thousand years or more. Granite does eventually decompose, but it takes a very long time.

On Wednesday April 11 we left Aurangabad, on a morning train; so crowded that we shoved Joanne into the women's compartment, with our rucksacks, and then we fought our way into the regular bogies, at one point almost afraid we couldn't even get into the train. It eased up a bit farther down the line. At 11 A.M. we were at the trunk-line junction, where the big trains run between Delhi and Bombay, and caught another train that got us into Bombay by six in the evening. Allen Ginsberg had a contact from New York, an ex–Bryn Mawr girl living in Bombay, Radhika Jayakar. He phoned her—at first she wasn't in—so I took my map and bearings, and leaving the others to wait in the Victoria Station, found my way on foot to the office of the Messageries Maritimes, to pick up mail and verify our ship—it was sailing from Bombay (on its way from Marseille) April 21, and would be the same ship again, the *Cambodge*.

XXV. *Bombay*

RADHIKA JAYAKAR is a tiny young woman with an elegant figure, whose parents are well situated. She said we could stay in their apartment, which was the whole first floor of a large building, as long as we liked—gave us a big room furnished in a curiously Indian-Japanese synthesis of styles, with the fans going constantly. The Jayakars live on Malabar Hill, the best district I gather in Bombay, and the first time in India we had seen anything remotely approaching the look and feel of a Western city, or a Western-type residential district with planted trees and apartment houses and nice streets up and down hillsides. Bombay immediately had a nice feeling for us. And it was a great relief to be at the end of our train travel, since we were now carrying more luggage than we had begun with—shopping, and books.

At the American Express we had a note waiting for us from the Australian fellow we'd met on the ship, Neale Hunter. He had gotten off the ship in Singapore, gone up through Malaya and across by deck-class freighter to Madras, then hitchhiked north to Calcutta and across India to Bombay. In his note he said he was living for a few weeks in a palm-frond hut at Juhu Beach. Next morning, getting the route to Juhu Beach from Radhika (who was busy that day), the four of us rode buses to Juhu, found the right section of beach, and the little hut he'd built, with his rucksack all packed in it. After while he came back, with another fellow (American) he'd met on the road. They had both been camping on the beach two weeks, but were about to hitchhike to Poona. It was fun meeting him in such a strange place—we swam in the Arabian sea, leaving our stuff in his hut (which he said was safe because he had left his stuff in it unguarded many times in the previous two weeks) and when we got back found out that we'd been hit—Neale lost his camera from Japan, and I lost the money in my wallet (about $10 in Indian rupees), my watch—a banged up cheap Swiss watch that John the Dutchman had given me when he left Kyoto—and my Swiss Army jackknife, which is the one thing I was sorry to see go. Luckily Allen G.'s wallet, with his passport and 150 Rupees was untouched, and so was Joanne's camera, which was in an open bag. It was our only contribution to thieves in India, so I figure we got off fairly easy. Joanne let me have her Boy Scout knife to use.

Ginsberg had some North African pot he'd been carrying around for some time so we sat on the sand and got high—first time for Neale, and he was quite astounded by it all. North African stuff is strong. Then at twilight he and his friend put on their packs and started down the road, and we caught a bus back to Bombay.

Radhika's mother is a celebrated lady Indian writer and intellectual. She writes short stories in English under the name of Pupul Jayakar. She is also in the government cottage-industries work, and went to New York two years ago to see about sending hand-woven madras to the States (the project fell through because of the opposition of American business). She had been touring Orissa checking the handicrafts there, and came back to Bombay now. A short, intense, talkative woman. Divorced. Her own mother (Radhika's grandmother), who lived in a house across the street, also a powerful intellectual old lady. Most of the time Mrs. Jayakar lives in her apartment in New Delhi, where her work is.

The whole Jayakar family follows Krishnamurti. He stays in their house when he passes through Bombay. They had some striking photographs of him around and on the wall. So, by extension, they had some interest in Zen, which led to several very interesting conversations. Krishnamurti says he teaches nothing but "absolute, unconditioned freedom." This sounds like Zen, and indeed Buddhism; but he adds that absolutely no discipline, no method, of any sort can lead to this freedom. He means it quite literally, so there is nothing for his followers to do. Zen, as a whole, asserts that effort or method won't help you, but you've got to try. By this paradoxical bind they achieve some results. Krishnamurti does talk about "Mind enquiry" though, which sounds rather similar to Ramana Maharshi's self-enquiry. Less orthodoxly Hindu. Krishnamurti has a surprisingly large following among Indian intellectuals, especially those who are not of the Gandhian social-work bent.

Night of April 13, a concert on the night of Rama's birthday; Kathak dancing, a sitar, some singers. None so good.

Ramana Maharshi on drugs (quoted to us by a man who had studied with him in the thirties, named Maurice Freedman): "They confer real experiences and insights, but they are useless, for one has not fulfilled the preliminary conditions."

We live a comfortable, easy life in Bombay, in clean and beautiful quarters, getting a view of the country we hadn't so far seen. Mangoes are just in season, the famous "alphonso" mangoes of Bombay which have no stringiness and are very sweet. There is nothing in the world as delicious as a good mango. And we eat ripe bananas. Bombay downtown has the best variety of eating places in India, and since there is

Karla Caves, Chaitya (stupa) chamber.

little caste-consciousness one can find a wide variety of foods—Mogul cooking, Parsi cooking, some of the best. Radhika Jayakar does half an hour of yoga exercises every morning, and the whole family is vegetarian. Another night, we go to a concert, of Ali Akbar Khan and Chattur Lal, again. They aren't quite so good this time, though, because tired. So later Chattur Lal (the next night that is) calls us at 9 P.M. and asks if we want to sit in on a private session. We go to an apartment downtown, and he's playing together with the woman sarod-player we'd heard him play with first. About 40 people crowded in, sitting on the floor. They are really swinging this time. We walked halfway back to Malabar hill along the water's edge.

April 17, took a one-day trip by train to the Karla caves, a very early Buddhist cave-temple, all Hinayana. The largest single cave of all is there; and it is probably the most perfect, architecturally. It has a 100-foot? high barrel-ceiling, with ribs cut to look like the wooden ribs in the original wooden structure it is meant to look like. To the right and left of the entrance are bas-relief panels of life-size couples, their arms around each other's backs or waists, facing out—the women richly breasted and nude, the men in complex loincloths; they are commonly explained as being statues of the couples who donated money to help build the cave. Karla is up to 1800 feet high on the Deccan plateau, again a sort of Nevada or Utah landscape. Back down in the evening to Bombay, which is moist and warm, and has green.

Karla Caves donor couple.

April 18 we gave a poetry reading by request on the roof of an apartment house to a large group of Bombay intelligentsia (the American consul is there). Then went to the apartment of an Indian Jew (they have an ancient colony on the Malabar coast) named Nissim Ezekial, who is one of the leading figures in Indian English-language poetry. After hearing three young men read their English-language poetry, we had to explain to them that if they insisted on writing in English like Englishmen who in India would listen? All their poems smelled like Oxford. They in turn, didn't think much of our poetry, I suspect—we were too far from the English Literary Tradition to be acceptable to them.

On the 20th Radhika and us, and also Hope Savage, who had turned up in Bombay in her shawl and barefoot, all went swimming at Juhu beach. The water is *really* lukewarm. Peter and I running up and down the beach, and I did my first handspring in my whole life. I was so surprised I tried it several more times, and succeeded twice. They weren't perfect or graceful though. Radhika explained that the tattoo on my left leg is not *Aum*, as I had thought, but *Pranava*, which is a "magical name of Aum." It's very beneficial.—Rolled over and over by sloppy little hot waves.

Now we are about to leave India, and feeling very lucky to have come through it all intact, with nothing worse than diarrhea a few times, quite elated really. And glad to be leaving, then, because India is not comfortable, nor is the food really good enough to stay healthy on forever. If you were settled in one spot and could do your own cooking and fix up your own quarters to suit yourself it would be different, of course.

But India in any case is not a comfortable country, the way Japan is. The contrasts are very sharp. Japanese culture is basically hedonistic, and even at its poorest, provides comforts: like the universal public baths, where you can get all the hot water you want to wash yourself clean, any time of the year. Cleanliness. Clean houses, clean inns, no matter how inexpensive. Toilet paper. (India doesn't use toilet paper, in part, because no one can *afford* it!) And of course, bars, sake stalls, teahouses, young pretty girl hostesses, all that sort of thing—which exists in limited quantity in India, and is much more degraded and dirty than it is in Japan. To understand the problem in part just picture the consequences of having various groups of people who will not dine together, bathe together, or even use the same water supply. How can you have a public life with castes? In India we always bathed by standing near a tap and pouring pans of water over ourselves. In the country one does this by standing in a stream or pond; and it was not uncommon to see people standing in filthy murky-looking water pouring panful after panful over themselves happily washing. The public manners of Indians are much noisier and more argumentative than the Japanese too (and Japanese public manners are lots worse than private manners). Dishonesty, cheating, hostility, rudeness, loudness, thoughtlessness, etc., on all sides in India. Again perhaps part of being a country overrun by so many aggressors, and full of so many groups constantly confronting each other. Yet there is a kind of honesty in India which is ultimately lacking in Japan; straightforwardness though rude, and a general refusal to play roles.

There's nothing phony there (even the phony holy men are *really* doing ascetic practices, *really* celibate, *really* vegetarian; their phoniness is that their understanding may not be as great as people or their own literature ascribes to them). The people, the landscape, even the religion, sticks to essentials. Part of this is just the poverty and suffering, I suppose, which cannot be acted over. But more than that: even the poverty-stricken areas of Japan, or poor periods of history, never removed the constant playing of social roles by which Japanese society exists. I think the difference is simply that for the Japanese person (average) there is no substance or reality he can conceive of outside the social fabric. For the Indian, all reality is outside the social fabric, which exists at best as a kind of disciplinary religious system for laymen, so that if you follow it properly ultimately you'd be born into the Brahman caste and from there can be reborn into nonhuman higher realms. (For this reason Zen is very much an anomaly in Japan, and one can understand why it has never been seriously popular.)

For myself the worst thing in India was my bad temper. I became extremely short and easily roused, against real or imagined dirty tricks pulled on me. It sure is hard to travel around and keep all serene and tolerant. At least the Indians are sure of

Right:
Hope Savage.

Far right:
Radhika Jayakar.

who they are, and proud of it to the point of arrogance. They don't figure they have much to learn from the West outside of engineering and science; the Japanese really have a problem of what's my identity.

The Americans we saw in India all looked sleek, vaguely troubled, trying to be good guys, but uncomprehending (except the beatniks). Young Germans are everywhere, making a strong impression because of their poverty and independence and spiritedness.

April 21: Radhika in a white sari, full-blossomed like a classical Indian beauty, and Hope Savage in an aboriginal two-color dress and shawl, accompanied us with our baggage in two taxis to the dock. We had stripped down all we could, but still were well loaded—Joanne had left her high heels far behind and was moving with sure and accustomed techniques through all the travel routines—it was a marvel how she managed every time we pulled up for a night to do a laundry, wash her hair, write in her notebook, and study our next day's sightseeing without a hitch. We drank some bottles of mangola pop at the Ballard Pier Cafe, and they left us at the medical inspection hall on the pier. Joanne and I got in line for medical checks, while they turned back to walk into India. Joanne pretty in slacks and black blouse, all tan. We go through medical (i.e., have you got your vaccination certificates) and customs with no trouble at all; they don't even open our rucksacks. The ship sails at 6.

XXVI. Return Voyage

I HAD THREE Chinese men as roommates; Joanne was in with an Indian lady with a baby, who was later moved, leaving her all alone. The Chinese men were all on their way home to Peking: one had been in India thirty years as a small business-man—had left a wife and a small son behind; now he has grandchildren. I ask him, aren't you afraid to go to Communist China? He says yes. But it's China, and my family is there.

April 23, at Colombo. I had written the Canadian High Commissioner in Colombo, a Mr. James George, at the suggestion of a former student at the Kyoto Zen Institute. When the ship pulled in Colombo, I gave him a call, and he immediately sent the big black Canadian Commissioner car over to pick us up, flying a flag and driven by a driver. He took us to a Buddhist temple in Colombo we'd failed to see on our first stop here, the Kelaniya vihara, which had some extremely nice paintings in it, both old and new. The new ones showed conscious attempts to adopt Ajanta and Sigiriya styles to modern Buddhist art. The older paintings, recently cleaned up to be see-able, have a kicky goofiness to the Buddha-figures, with lots of design pat-terns and animals. Mr. George used to be a Gurdjieff man, who has recently become interested in Zen. He went up to visit the Ramana Maharshi Ashram last winter, and knows all the gossip about the main Buddhist and Hindu teachers in India and

Ceylon. He took us to his mansion for dinner, which was pretty good although the silverware and servants were even more impressive, and the real imported liquors he served too. All air-conditioned. His wife and children, like himself, curiously tall and slow-speaking and serious, but faintly hip. He may be stopping here in Kyoto in the future.

He described an Englishman who had poked around in Ceylon for sometime looking for wisdom, and was about to give it up and go back. One day he was in the town of Jaffna browsing in a bookstore, in the section on Oriental philosophy. A ragged old Ceylonese man came up to him and said, "Bloody fool, it's not in books!" and walked out. He located the man later and turned out he was known locally as Yogaswami; became the disciple of the old man for some time.

Limousine takes us back to the pier and we ride the launch out to the ship. Next day, ashore again in Colombo, visited the museum and dug 200-year-old styles of fabric design. 28 April: Singapore—a tiresome place, I still say.

1 May: Saigon—quieter than before; the Viet Cong were getting more serious; the museum interesting because in one room Indian art, in the next Chinese, we could look at them together—part of the difference between the genius of wood and the genius of stone. Far Eastern wood carvings glow with muted coloring—are alive-looking, this-worldly—as against Indian super-brilliant painted stone figures, colors of Disneyland heaven. One thing I learned: religion isn't necessarily art; the vulgarity

of modern Indian religious iconography does not really detract from its seriousness. Japanese Buddhism is 9/10ths aestheticism.

4 May: Hong Kong: Five scrolls, reproductions of Sung Dynasty masterpieces, made by multi-woodblock process and mounted—all done in Peking, one of the world's major publishing centers—and a great meal of braised duck, sweet and sour pork, beef slice w/ fried noodles, a bottle of Chinese wine, hundred-year eggs. Joanne wearing her striped handloomed Punjabi dress. (I can't forget the face of Chattur Lal swinging and swaying and grimacing with his tabla—Ali Akbar with closed eyes dreaming out his world of sound.) Mr. Wang, my Chinese roommate, disembarks. In eight days, he says, he'll be in Peking. Back to sea: at our table a jolly fat Welshman named Derek Bosley, and a Swiss boy. Derek is a chief engineer by trade, taking a vacation to go visit his girl friend in Osaka. The Swiss is going to Tokyo for a year to study judo. I ask him if he will teach judo when he gets back—he says no, he is a potter, but he wanted to study judo just for himself. Going home I read the *Jataka Tales*, the *Bhagavad Gita* again, a history of Himalayan mountaineering called *Abode of Snow*; two books on Tibetan religion. Eight May (my birthday) docked at Kobe. Carrying our own gear walked off the ship, checked out through customs, took a taxi to the Kobe station, and took the Kyoto fast electric express, an hour to Kyoto; took a taxi to our front door. Mrs. Hosaka, the old lady who lives on the second floor, was expecting us; the house was clean as we left it.

25 August 1962, and I finish this account. Allen Ginsberg and Peter later went to Calcutta, Allen got into Sikkim, and walked a day and a half over the hills from Gangtok to the new monastery of Dudjom Rimpoche, the Dalai Lama's translator's teacher—who promised to give Allen some wangs ("powers") if he'd come back this fall and meditate awhile.

HAIL THE LORD OF THE THREE WORLDS

Bibliographical Notes

For bibliography, A. L. Basham's *The Wonder That Was India* (Grove Press paperback) is fascinating and scholarly. For post-Muslim and British history, I suppose V. A. Smith's *Oxford History of India* is as good as anything. McKim Marriot (ed.) is excellent for contemporary village life, both north and south. The Pelican, Benjamin Rowland, *Art and Architecture of India,* and the Bollingen series two-volume Zimmer *Art of Indian Asia.* Helmut Hoffman, *The Religions of Tibet* (George Allen & Unwin), and Madame Alexandra David-Neel, *The Secret Oral Teachings in Tibetan Buddhist Sects* (the latter is a great, incisive, little book—far better than the title allows). Lama Anagarika Govinda *op. cit.* Bhikku Nyanapondika *op. cit.* Gandhi, *My Experiments with Truth* (autobiography).

Printed in the United States
by Baker & Taylor Publisher Services